ROOKIE COOKING

ROOKIE COOKING

EVERY GREAT COOK HAS TO START SOMEWHERE

CHEF JIM EDWARDS

Photographs by Ted Axelrod

Skyhorse Publishing

Skyhorse Publishing books may be purchased in bulk at special discounts for sales promotion, corporate gifts, fund-raising, or educational purposes. Special editions can also be created to specifications. For details, contact the Special Sales Department, Skyhorse Publishing, 307 West 36th Street, 11th Floor, New York, NY 10018 or info@skyhorsepublishing.com.

Skyhorse® and Skyhorse Publishing® are registered trademarks of Skyhorse Publishing, Inc.®, a Delaware corporation.

Visit our website at www.skyhorsepublishing.com.

10 9 8 7 6 5 4 3 2 1

Library of Congress Cataloging-in-Publication Data is available on file.

Cover design by Jane Sheppard
Cover image: iStockphoto

Print ISBN: 978-1-5107-1165-5
Ebook ISBN: 978-1-5107-1166-2

Printed in China

CONTENTS

This book is dedicated to my grandmother, Lucy Oliveri, who opened my eyes to the exciting world of food and cooking when I was a young boy. Grandma cooked everything from scratch with ingredients that she grew and raised herself; she had fruit trees and a massive vegetable garden. Produce that was not used during the season was canned for use during the winter. She raised chickens, turkeys, and a pig each year. In the mornings, my siblings and I would go into the hen house to fight the mother hens over their eggs. She did all that without using recipes, and she was the best from-scratch cook I have ever known.

PART ONE

SETTING UP YOUR KITCHEN AND PANTRY

CHAPTER ONE

Sanitation, Food Safety, and Labels

Basics of Staying Safe

While cooking can be a truly rewarding experience, there are certain hazards that are inherent to the process. Anyone who spends time in the kitchen must have a working knowledge of these hazards in order to ensure their own safety and the safety of those they are cooking for. Some of these hazards are apparent and others are not. We will explore both in order to enhance your awareness and make your cooking experience a safe and rewarding one.

The two most obvious hazards in the kitchen are cutting and burning hazards. These are largely hazardous to the cook and not the guests. In a commercial kitchen, chefs and cooks protect themselves from these types of hazards by first wearing the proper clothing. Long pants and closed-toe shoes (not sandals) will afford the cook an added layer of protection in case a knife is dropped or hot liquid is spilled. Since the home cook is in it for the fun of it, these guidelines may or may not apply but they are worth mentioning in the context of personal protection.

Protection against burning also includes the use of temperature resistant pot holders when handling hot pots and pans. When moving hot pans in and out of the oven, oven mitts with a high rf or insulation factor will afford maximum protection. These should ideally cover as much of the arm as possible. Many of the worst burns occur when the back of the hand or the arm comes in contact with an oven rack that is above the item you are working with. Never use a wet oven mitt, towel, or pot holder to handle hot pans. The steam generated from the contact with the pan can cause serious burns. Some mitts and pot holders, such as silicone coated varieties are resistant to heat and spills, which means that hot oil or water that comes in contact with the mitt will not be absorbed, avoiding a burn. No matter how careful you are, occasionally all cooks suffer burns. When this happens, the affected area should be immediately cooled with ice to suppress the burn.

A sharp knife is perhaps the tool that is most frequently used in the kitchen. Knives are not, however, the only potential cutting hazard. Other devices like mandolines can also pose a risk to the operator, especially if they are not properly protected. Many adult cooking schools offer classes in proper and safe knife skills, and the rookie cook in particular should consider taking one of these classes. Additionally, cooks can wear a protective cut glove when using a knife or mandoline; a practice that many food service management companies require of all employees. A further discussion of knives and their use takes place in Chapters 4 and 6 of this section.

Food contamination poses a potential health threat to both the cook and the guests. Food contamination, comes in three forms: physical contamination, chemical contamination and biological contamination. Physical contamination occurs when foreign objects are mixed with food. These objects can come from several sources and therefore have different means of minimizing or eliminating them as contaminants. The most common sources are administrative or stationery items such as paper clips, rubber bands, pens, pencils, and thumb tacks; food contact vessels, like worn out or rusty pots and pans, chipped plates or splintered wood; and animal sources—either human or pet—such as fingernails, hair, bandages, and bodily fluids.

Separating administrative items from the working area of the kitchen is the obvious means of eliminating administrative or stationary contamination. While it may sometimes be helpful to have a means of jotting down ideas or recipes, it is also a good idea to keep these items in a separate area of the kitchen. Food itself, especially wrappers and binders, can also become a source of this type of contamination. Thoroughly check fresh vegetables for rubber bands and other binders and discard them before processing the vegetables.

Any food contact surface that is made of wood requires special attention so as not to introduce splinters to the food. Wooden cutting boards need to be oiled regularly with mineral oil. Wooden spoons or bowls need to be discarded when chipped or cracked. Enameled pots that are worn through need to be similarly discarded. Cast iron cookware needs periodic seasoning to eliminate rust contamination. Glass or porcelain plates, bowls, and glasses should be discarded if chipped.

Physical contaminants from animal sources can be eliminated through common sense. Anyone who wishes to become a serious cook should understand the importance of using hair restraint while cooking. The general rule is if your hair touches your shoulders, you should use some form of hair restraint, either a cap or a hair tie. Animal hair can be excluded from food by not allowing pets in the kitchen while you're cooking and not petting or otherwise handling them during these times. Keep fingernails well groomed. If you have a cut or wound on your hand, cover it with a bandage and then cover the bandage with a disposable food service glove.

The chief sources of chemical contamination in the kitchen are cleaning and sanitation supplies and pesticides. The most efficient way of eliminating these items as food contaminants is proper storage. Pesticides and sanitation supplies should never be stored in a cabinet that is also used to store food. The most logical place to store sanitation supplies is under the sink, since this is the area of the kitchen where they are generally used. Pesticides should not be stored in any kitchen area. In the rare instance when it becomes necessary to use a pesticide in a food service area, there should be a period of down time between their use and food preparation. All food contact surfaces should be thoroughly cleaned before returning the area to food prep.

Biological contamination is the single most common source of food borne illness and therefore requires a more thorough examination. For this discussion, we will define what potentially hazardous food is and describe ways in which a cook can minimize their risk of contracting food borne illness.

It is estimated that there are 70 million cases of food borne illness in the US each year. Many of these incidents are never reported or they are passed off as a "twenty-four hour virus." Unfortunately, over five thousand of these cases result in death. In almost every case, food borne illness is the result of improper handling, storage, or cooking of food.

Potentially hazardous food (PHF) is any food with a pH of greater than 4.5 and/or a water activity of 0.85 or greater. In addition, foods with high protein content, a history of being involved in food borne illness, or a natural potential for contamination due to production and processing methods should be considered PHF. A partial list of PHF includes: fish, shellfish and crustaceans; poultry, meat, milk, and milk products; shelled eggs; tofu or other soy protein food; sprouts and raw seeds; sliced melons; baked or boiled potatoes; cooked rice, beans, or other heat-treated food; garlic-in-oil mixtures; and synthetic ingredients, such as texture soy protein and meat alternatives.

Hand Washing

Improper hand washing has been identified as the number one source of food borne illness. Food borne pathogens use improperly washed hands as a transport system to food. Hands should be washed in the following manner. Wet hands with running water as hot as you can stand it (at least 100°F). Apply soap. Vigorously scrub hands and arms for at least twenty seconds. Clean under fingernails and between fingers, using a brush. Rinse thoroughly under running water. Dry hands and arms with a single-use paper towel.

Instances when you should wash hands are: before and after handling raw meat, fish, or eggs; after using the rest room; after sneezing, coughing, or using a handkerchief or tissue;; after smoking, drinking, eating, or chewing gum or tobacco; after handling chemicals that might affect the safety of food; after handling garbage.

Wearing disposable gloves can afford an extra level of safety in handling food. In no instances, however, should wearing gloves replace proper hand washing. Gloves should be worn when handling any food that is ready to eat. Food ready to eat is food that will not be cooked between the time you touch it and someone eats it. This could be a cold item like a salad or merely food that is being plated after cooking. Gloves should also be worn when handling raw meat, fish, eggs or other potentially hazardous food, and when there is a cut or open sore on the hands. Gloves should not replace bandages, but must be worn over a properly bandaged cut or sore. That way, bandages and/or bodily fluids do not end up in food. Gloves should not be worn to perform more than one task and should be discarded after each individual task.

Time Temperature Abuse

Food has been Time Temperature abused any time it has been allowed to remain too long at temperatures that are favorable to the growth of food borne microorganisms. The temperature range of 41°F to 135°F has been identified as the Food Temperature Danger Zone. Potentially hazardous food should not be exposed to this temperature for more than four hours. It is important to recognize that this exposure is cumulative. Therefore, the length of time that food is exposed to this temperature during each step in the process of purchasing, storing, thawing, preparing, cooking, holding, and serving food must be added together to determine the total exposure.

Storage areas for perishable food should be equipped with a reliable thermometer to monitor the temperature of each zone, i.e. refrigerators and freezers. Refrigerator temperatures should remain between 34° and 41°F. Freezer temperatures should be 0°F or less. Do not overload storage areas. Perishable food should be discarded after seven days in a refrigerator. All food should be used in the order it was purchased (first in; first out).

There are only four acceptable ways to defrost frozen food: in a refrigerator at 41°F or less; submerged in running potable water at 70°F or less; in a microwave oven, if the food will be immediately cooked; directly cooked if the food item is less than three pounds.

When prepping perishable food for serving or cooking, work in small quantities, removing only what will be processed in thirty minutes. Never place hot food in a refrigerator. Cool the food in shallow trays or dishes in a cold water bath. Food should be cooled from 140°F to 75°F in less than two hours and from 75°F to less than 41°F in two hours or less. It is important to cook meat, fish, and eggs to a minimum internal temperature in order to avoid food borne illness.

The internal temperature of all cooked potentially hazardous food should be measured by using a reliable, calibrated meat thermometer. Temperatures should be measured in the thickest part of the item, not on a bone.

Cooking Chart for Meat, Fish, Poultry, and Eggs

Item	Minimum Internal Temp.
Beef (whole cuts)	145°
Pork (whole cuts)	145°
Lamb (whole cuts)	145°
Fish (whole or filet)	145°
Veal (whole cuts)	145°
Eggs	145°
Ground Meat or Fish (other than poultry)	155°
Poultry	165°
Stuffing	165°

Food should be reheated to 165°F in less than two hours. Any hot food held for serving should be held above 140°F. Cold food held for serving should be held at less than 41°F.

Cross-Contamination

Cross-contamination occurs when microorganisms are transferred from one surface or food to another. Common examples of cross-contamination are:

- Adding raw contaminated ingredients to food that requires no further cooking.
- Food contact surfaces, such as cutting boards that are not cleaned and sanitized before touching cooked or ready to eat food.
- Allowing raw food to touch or drip fluids into cooked or ready to eat food.
- Hands that touch contaminated or raw food and then come in contact with cooked or ready to eat food.
- Contaminated cleaning cloths that are not cleaned and sanitized before being used on other food-contact surfaces.

Cutting boards should be washed and sanitized between uses. Clean boards may be sanitized by immersing them in a solution of one tablespoon bleach to one gallon water for at least thirty seconds. Spray disinfectant cleaners may be used on clean boards that are too large to fit into a sink. Wooden cutting boards should be treated with mineral oil after cleaning, sanitizing, and drying. Cutting boards with cracks or large gaps should be discarded as the cracks or gaps harbor bacteria and pose a contamination hazard.

Raw meats and other potentially hazardous food should never be stored above cooked or ready to eat food. Raw meat or fish should be stored in a drip pan. To store a variety of raw meats or fish, use the cooking chart for minimum internal cooking temperature to determine which items have the highest and lowest minimums. Store items from top to bottom in ascending order of minimum internal cooking temperature, e.g., store beef above chicken.

Proper hand washing and use of disposable gloves will help to minimize the risk of cross-contamination from hands to food. Disposable gloves should be worn whenever handling potentially hazardous food. Disposable gloves should be worn whenever touching cooked or ready to eat food.

Whenever possible, disposable cloths and towels should be used for cleaning and sanitizing. Reusable towels that come in contact with surfaces that are con-taminated should be sanitized in a bleach solution before reuse.

The following is a list of sanitation supplies that should be on hand in the kitchen:

- Bleach
- Disposable food service gloves
- Disposable sanitary wipes
- Dish detergent
- Scrubby sponge
- Bar Keepers Friend to scrub pots
- Mineral oil for oiling wooden cutting boards

Food Labels and Nomenclature

In order to become a cook, one must have a working knowledge of two things: cook's ingredients and cooking techniques. We will explore both of these issues. First, a bit of background information on food labels and nomenclature.

During the past three decades, the consumer has become increasingly informed and concerned about the food they eat. In rapidly growing numbers, today's consumer is rejecting the status quo of factory farming and opting for local ingredients that are grown or raised under specific guidelines that ensure quality. This increased demand for accountability on the part of farmers, food processors and manufacturers, and food professionals has produced a "new" food industry that resembles in most part the old way of putting food on the table (before supermarkets and mass transportation of food from around the country and around the world). With these changes come new ways to package, label, and distribute the food that we eat. Not all of these new terms and labels are fully understood by consumers. The following passages are an attempt to sort out some of the nomenclature that consumers see on today's food labels.

Understanding Food Labels

The FDA has, over the past few decades, improved the quality and safety of the American food supply by establishing labeling standards for all packaged food. According to law, all packaged food must display the weight of the product, ingredients in the product, and a breakdown of the nutritional analysis. Ingredients are always listed in order of abundance, so that the most abundant ingredient in the product is listed first and the least abundant is listed last. That way, the consumer can read the ingredient list and determine whether or not a specific ingredient in the product is present in high or low quantity.

Nutritional data must contain the following information: serving size; number of servings per container, and nutritional breakdown. The serving size can sometimes be misleading because it has a direct impact on the nutritional data. If the serving size is too small, the nutritional data may become so skewed that it loses relevance to the user. That's why it's a good idea to look at the size of the container and see if you think the serving size and therefore number of servings per container is a reasonable representation of what you might eat in one serving. If it is too small in your mind, then you will need to multiply the nutritional data by whatever factor you think results in a reasonable serving size.

Nutritional data contains a breakdown of the nutritional content of the food in the package. The specific categories are calories per serving; calories from fat; a breakdown of the types of fat (saturated; unsaturated, etc.); calories from carbohydrates; and calories from protein. There is an additional number for each that describes the percent of RDA (recommended daily allowance) each category provides to the "average" person. Additional nutritional data may include

vitamin and mineral breakdown and fiber content, each also accompanied by a percent of RDA.

All Natural Food

The term "natural" or "all natural" that has increasingly shown up on food labels is one that defies definition. While the consumer might think that food with these words on the label is healthier for them, this may or may not be the truth. Since the vast majority of food is derived from natural products of plants and animals, defining the term "natural" becomes problematic. In actuality, there is no legal definition of the term natural in the United States. It may be assumed that "all natural" foods have little or no artificial ingredients, little processing, and no hormones, antibiotics, or food colorings, but since there are no legal guidelines, almost anything may contain the word "natural" on the label.

Organic and Certified Organic

According to the National Organic Standards Board, "Organic agriculture is an ecological production management system that promotes and enhances biodiversity, biological cycles and soil biological activity. It is based on minimal use of off-farm inputs and on management practices that restore, maintain, and enhance ecological harmony." Additionally, organic farming maintains and replenishes soil fertility without the use of toxic chemicals like pesticides, fertilizers, and herbicides. Largely due to consumer concerns about food safety and nutrition, the organic food industry has grown from a $1 billion industry in 1990 to a $23.6 billion dollar industry in 2008.

The process of certification for organic farmers includes several steps. These include:

- Avoidance of use of chemical fertilizers, pesticides, antibiotics and hormones, irradiation, and genetically altered organisms.
- Use of chemical-free farmland. Usually the organic farmer must wait three years to start organic farming on an existing non-organic operation.
- Maintaining records for production and sales
- Physical separation of organic and non-organic processes.
- On-site inspections.

The US government defines three levels of organic food with three different labeling guidelines: Products made entirely of certified organic ingredients may carry the label "100% Organic"; products with at least 95 percent organic ingredients can carry the label "organic" (both may carry the USDA organic seal); products comprised of at least 70 percent organic ingredients may be labeled "made with organic ingredients"; and products with less than 70 percent organic ingredients may state so in the ingredient list but nowhere else on the label.

In the US, the certification process is handled by state, non-profit, and private organizations. The California Certified Organic Farmers was one of the first organizations to carry out the certification process in the US. Other private organizations like CCOF and the Organic Trade Organization currently offer certification assistance for farmers. The process is much the same as described above. Farmers must wait a period of time (usually three years) before converting non-organic farms to organic; they must outline and document the procedures for conversion; they must maintain detailed records; they must undergo periodic site inspections and soil analysis; and they must pay a fee to the agency (usually $400–$2,000 per year).

The last detail—paying a fee to an agency to become certified—and the fact that organic certification is subject to government guidelines and federal law, has many small farmers and practitioners wary of the system. In short, any time a law is passed and a set of guidelines are part of that law, any organization with the means and will to hire lobbyists can attempt to implement loopholes and exemptions to that law, thereby diluting or outright corrupting its original intent.

Due the aforementioned factors, many independent farmers have become wary of the organic certification process and view it as a possible means of driving the small farmer out of business and corrupting the quality of organic food. Some of the post-Depression practitioners remember the early days of modern organic farming, when certification was based on the honor system. They see the government and other certification bodies as creating too much red tape and additional costs for the small farmer to compete. Their main concern is that the food factories that are owned and operated by big business may successfully lobby congress to pass amendments and exemptions to the current laws, thereby clouding the line that currently separates organic farming from factory farming.

One alternative to certification as organic is the Participatory Guarantee System. These are small groups of local participants who operate on trust, social networking, and knowledge exchange in much the same way as they did in the old days. This system allows participants to choose and define standards based upon local issues, develop and implement certification of these standards, and take part in certification decisions.

Cage Free

There is probably no other term in modern food labeling with as much controversy attached to it as the words cage free. This applies, of course, to chickens, especially laying hens, but also to meat chickens. The original intent of those who espoused returning to the old ways of raising chickens was ethically driven. It's no secret that chickens raised in so called "battery cages" are subjected to perhaps the most inhumane treatment of all livestock. In the end, of course, they all end up being slaughtered for consumption, either by humans or by other animal species in the form of animal feed. It's their treatment while alive that has many people up in arms.

Although cage free chickens may be housed inside with sometimes thousands of chickens in a small space, there are some ethical advantages over battery caging. Cage free chickens are allowed to spread their wings, nest and walk, albeit in a confined space. These are all vital natural behaviors for chickens and this alone affords them a better quality of life than battery caged chickens. While raising chickens in a cage free environment does not necessarily mean that the system is humane, it is a step in the right direction.

Free Range

Although the words "Free Range" may appear on other food labels, the USDA applies this term only to the raising of poultry. In their words, the definition of free range is "Producers must demonstrate to the Agency that the poultry has been allowed access to the outside." The problem with this definition lies in the interpretation and application. There are no guidelines for the quality or size of the outside area and none for the duration per day that the chickens should be outside. That lack of guidelines produces a myriad of results in practice. Some free range chickens have small doors leading to a small area covered with gravel. Others have continuous access to shaded grassy areas.

Free range livestock management is not a new concept. Before the development of barbed wire and chicken wire, ranchers herded their livestock to allow them a varied diet and fight disease. Chickens were raised outside where the sunlight provided vital Vitamin D. This method of raising poultry was practiced in large flocks until the 1950s. After the discovery of Vitamins A and D in the 1920s researchers began to develop a better understanding of the impact of nutrition on raising livestock. Supplements of both nutrients allowed them to develop the current system, where poultry need not see the light of day in order to get their proper vitamins.

Other Terms

With so many stamps and labels on food packaging, it's hard to imagine that food producers would come up with new ways to describe their products. For a number of reasons, they have. Since the list of organic farmers who have concerns about the certification process is growing, organizations like Certified Naturally Grown are offering small farmers an alternative to the USDA approved labeling as a "non-profit eco-labeling program." Since only farms that have gone through the certification process can legally display the "organic" label on their products, some are opting for using other terms like "authentic" and "natural."

Since there are no laws determining the prerequisites for putting free range on products other than eggs and poultry, the beef industry uses it largely as a marketing tool. Other terms that you may see on beef are "low stocking density," "pasture-raised," "grass fed," "old-fashioned," and "humanely raised." While the consumer may make certain assumptions about the way the beef was raised and slaughtered, again, there are no laws governing the use of any of these terms on labels, so they are used strictly as marketing tools.

At the top end of the animal humanitarianism scale is the "Free Farmed" label that is trademarked by the American Humane Association. It is considered to be the most rigorous of all labeling requirements as it strives to eliminate hunger, unnecessary fear, and pain in livestock. The certification process includes an initial inspection and periodic reinspections.

There are many other labels suggesting humane, eco-friendly, or otherwise responsible practices on the part of the farmer. These include "Hormone-Free," "Protested Harvest," "Salmon-Safe," and "Predator Friendly." While they are not recognized as official terms by any government agency, they are regulated by independent verification bodies that ensure the practices by which the food is harvested.

The issues with respect to food labeling will probably not get better for consumers and may even get worse. It is a bit sad, since consumers use terms like "organic" and "free range" to identify products in much the same way they might view "low fat" or "100% whole wheat." As economic concerns overshadow ethical concerns, more confusing terminology is likely to surface on food labels. The only way for consumers to truly know what they are eating is to read labels, ask questions about terms that are unfamiliar, and depend on multiple sources for up-to-date information. Any of these labels can be researched on the web. The Consumer's Guide to Environmental Labels rates almost all eco-labels.

CHAPTER TWO

Equipment and Tools

The Stove, Oven, and Microwave

The stove is the center of all cooking in a kitchen. Oftentimes the stove and kitchen are the focal points of social gatherings. In days gone by, fireplaces and wood burning stoves were the most popular heat source for home cooking. Today, they are largely used as a supplementary heat source during the winter, a feature that was merely a by-product of the cooking process in the old days. To a lesser degree, oil and coal burning stoves and ovens were used for cooking prior to the availability of gas and electricity. There are still several coal burning pizza ovens in operation in restaurants. In very old times, villages in Europe had wood burning baking ovens in the center of the town. A fire would be started once a week or so and the townspeople would bake their bread in community fashion, using only the residual heat of the brick and stone. It is this type of activity that united everyone and gave them a sense of being part of the community.

Beginning in the twentieth century, compressed natural gas and electricity began to replace wood as the chief source of energy for home stoves. They have since become the overwhelming favorites of modern America. The capacity of both stoves is rated by the number of BTU's (British Thermal Units) generated by the various heated zones. The higher the BTU rating, the quicker and hotter the heat source is. A typical home range has a BTU rating of 5,000 to 8,000. The more sophisticated home ranges like Viking, Thermidor, Dacor, and Wolf have a BTU rating of 15,000 per burner and more.

Electric ranges and ovens are the most popular type of heat source for the American home kitchen. They are relatively inexpensive to purchase and operate. Since electricity is more readily available than gas, a factor that is becoming increasingly true in newer housing areas, electricity is preferred over gas. Ceramic surface electric ranges are becoming more popular than the classic coil type due to two factors, appearance and ease of operation. The standard heat coil is still present beneath the ceramic surface. The disadvantage of electric cooktops is their slow response time, both in heating and cooling. Many people who are used to cooking on gas also complain about the absence of a visible flame with electric, thereby forcing the user to rely on a numerical heat setting rather than the intensity of the flame to determine the proper temperature setting. Electric ovens, however are generally better for baking since there is no flame cycling on and off to make the air in the oven dry.

Gas ranges are the preferred heat source for most professional cooks and many home cooks. The two main reasons for this are response time in heating and cooling and the presence of a visible flame. Most people find it easier to determine the intensity of the heat by looking at the flame. The other main advantage of gas ranges is that models with higher BTU ratings than electric are available (for a fee). This makes gas ranges more suitable than electric for high temperature cooking techniques like sautéing and grilling.

Many areas do not have available natural gas utilities, making gas ranges less popular than electric. Some people who live in such areas opt to use compressed propane rather than natural gas. In these instances, special jets are installed on the unit. You should never try to use propane on a gas stove that is fitted with standard natural gas jets. Even with the special jets, compressed propane does not burn as clean or as hot as natural gas. In both the case of natural and compressed gas stoves, it is important to operate them with proper ventilation in the form of an exhaust hood. Hoods are always recommended to control smoke, but they are essential from a safety standpoint when dealing with higher capacity stoves. Aside from controlling smoke they vent toxic fumes that are a by-product of the combustion process and they also help to contain the heat. If your kitchen is equipped with one of the high performance stoves mentioned above, it is also important to insulate the surfaces nearest to the stove to protect against fire.

A third source of energy for both home and commercial ranges is induction. **Induction ranges** were introduced in the US and Europe in the 1970s. Large US appliance manufacturers carried the line for several years and tried to promote them for commercial use. For these large companies the induction line represented a very small portion of their business. Since this small market share was financially insignificant, the US distributors dropped the line and induction cooktops virtually disappeared from the American market by the mid-eighties. In Europe, energy costs were much higher than in the US. Since induction ranges are 99 percent energy efficient as opposed to the 45–50 percent efficiency of gas and electric, induction ranges grew in popularity in Europe. Today, induction ranges outsell electric ranges in Europe.

This is how the induction range works. All sources of alternating electric current generate magnetic fields. This energy field is called induction. A circular induction field, usually generated by way of a coil, creates alternating positive and negative charged particles. When the user turns the burner of an induction range on, AC current is charged into an induction coil that is located directly under the ceramic cooktop. When a piece of induction ready cookware is placed on top of this burner, the molecules in the cookware begin colliding with one another, creating friction that heats the pan.

One of the advantages of induction is that the cooktop itself does not generate heat. While some heat is transferred back to the cooktop from the heated pan, it is generally insufficient to bake spills on the surface, making cleanup much easier. Since the cooktop does not generate heat or fumes, no hood is required. The major advantage of induction cooktops is response time and precision. Induction cooktops can boil water nearly twice as fast as a 15,000 BTU gas burner. More importantly, induction cooktops have a nearly immediate response to cooling. They are also extremely accurate in holding lower temperatures, eliminating the necessity of a double boiler for activities like tempering chocolate and making Hollandaise Sauce. The disadvantages are cost and necessity of using induction ready cookware. Induction ready cookware is paramagnetic, meaning that it is made of materials that are attracted by a magnet. About 50 percent of cookware sold in the US is induction ready.

For the dorm room or studio apartment kitchen, there are alternatives to purchasing a full blown range and/or oven. There are three types of single and sometimes double free standing burners available on the market—electric, gas, and induction. Induction is perhaps the preferred burner over the other two, as it generates no fumes or heat and therefore is more suitable for use in confined areas. Fagor induction ranges and free standing burners are available at a reasonable price. It should be noted that if induction is your choice, you will need to purchase induction ready cookware.

Most often, ovens are part of the same unit that houses a range. When choosing an oven, the following features should be considered. Temperature range: typically 170° to 500° covers the entire working range for the home cook. Convection: the convection function of an oven engages a fan to circulate the hot air. This is especially helpful when roasting. Self cleaning: most brands have departed from the "continuous cleaning" of days gone by in favor of self cleaning ovens. The self cleaning function locks the oven door for the entire cycle and super heats the oven to 700–900° to carbonize and burn off any spills. This cycle may generate considerable smoke, so it is always a good idea to wipe out the interior of the oven to remove bulk debris prior to engaging the self cleaning function and to turn on your hood during the cycle. Most manufacturers instruct you to remove the oven racks prior to self cleaning.

In all instances, it is important to monitor the temperature of your oven with a reliable oven thermometer. This is true of all temperature controlled zones in the kitchen, including refrigerators and freezers. When selecting an oven thermometer, choose one whose working range matches the temperature range of the oven and whose readout is bold and easy to read. There are also some oven thermometers whose readout may be placed outside the oven so that there is no need to open the oven door to get a reading. Remember that all ovens have a temperature fluctuation of plus or minus 25°. If your oven is reading consistently high or consistently low, you may wish to alter the temperature setting to account for this variation as opposed to calling a service engineer.

Just as there are alternatives to large ranges, for the space-challenged kitchen, there are alternatives to free standing or wall ovens. **Microwave ovens** were invented in the 1950s and made their public debut for most Americans at the 1964–65 World Fair in New York. They have since become an indispensable appliance in both the professional and home kitchen. They operate on a similar principle to the induction cooktop. Radiant energy created through electricity excites the water molecules in food, causing molecular movement and friction that generates heat. They are very inexpensive and they heat food very quickly.

They do not generate any heat of their own and are therefore safe to use without a hood. They are most suited to reheating food and melting raw materials like butter and chocolate. They are also one of the four approved ways to defrost food (as long as the food will be immediately cooked). The disadvantages of microwave ovens are that they sometimes heat items too quickly, especially high fat foods, and they often heat food unevenly. Therefore all potentially hazardous food that is reheated or cooked in a microwave should be heated to an internal temperature of 165°F.

Since their public debut a half-century ago, microwave ovens have come into their own as an indispensible heat source in the modern kitchen. Many models, like the Breville Quick Touch Microwave Oven have a myriad of settings that allow the user to input a personal menu for favorite foods, ensuring reliable and reproducible results. No longer just a device for reheating leftovers, the user can change the settings so the food they are cooking is not overcooked or under cooked.

Toaster ovens are another small appliance that have increasingly taken the place of their big brother in the home kitchen. They take up less space, are far cheaper and, like the microwave oven, have morphed into a true appliance that does far more than toast bagels or warm up pizza.

The Breville Smart Oven is a state-of-the-art counter top oven that can add large oven functionality to the space challenged kitchen. Large enough to fit ¼ sheet pans and six slices of toast, the Smart Oven has nine pre-set functions, a frozen food option, and temperature conversion capabilities. Because of the unique design, the user can bake a 13" pizza in the Smart Oven.

Refrigerators & Freezers

Refrigerators are possibly as important a piece of kitchen equipment as a stove or range. **Refrigerators and freezers** help to extend the shelf life of perishable goods and freezers in particular can be used for storing smaller portions of batch prepared food. There seems to be no limit to the functions of a modern refrigerator; from ice and water dispensers to self defrosting settings to models that can now brew a cup of coffee or hot soup. Some of the larger models come in two styles—either under/over or side by side—a reference to the placement of the freezer in relation to the refrigerator. The under/over configuration works best if you're storing larger and wider containers of food. The side by side means less bending over to access the freezer.

It is necessary to practice proper food handling in order to maximize the capabilities of a refrigerator or freezer. All food should be properly covered or wrapped so that it is not exposed to the air. This is especially true of frozen food. Vacuum sealing frozen food can increase the shelf life in the freezer threefold. All spills should be cleaned up expeditiously. Food should be no hotter than 70° when placing in a refrigerator or freezer. Placing hot food in a refrigerator or freezer, especially in large quantity, can overtax the compressor and in some cases, cause your unit to fail.

There are some great choices for under counter refrigerators and freezers for the space challenged kitchen. Frigidaire makes several under counter refrigerators, some of which have freezers incorporated in the same unit. For higher performance commercial models, manufacturers like Traulsen, Randel, True and Beveragaire offer a host of solutions to cold storage of perishable food. Just as in the case of ovens, you should monitor the internal temperature of your refrigerator and freezer with a reliable, easy to read thermometer whose temperature range matches that of the appliance. Refrigerator temperatures should be maintained between 34° and 41°, while freezer temperatures are optimum below 0°.

Useful Electric Tools on Your Counter

There are several small pieces of equipment that can make life easier for the home cook, especially those with limited kitchen space. **Rice cookers** are the preferred method for cooking rice in Chinese and Asian restaurants. Rice cookers are as infallible at cooking rice as the person who is measuring the ingredients. Rice cookers know when the rice is done and they cycle to hold the product warm. They can be purchased in a variety of sizes and functionalities. Zojirushi is the leader in manufacturing quality rice cookers for the home cook.

Slow cookers became part of the American kitchen several decades ago in response to the ever challenging schedules of modern working couples, singles, and families. Slow cookers prepare food in a manner that conforms to those schedules. They too have come a long way since the days of the Rival Crock Pot®. All-Clad makes a slow cooker that has three temperature settings, and extended cooking/delay up to twenty-six hours. Generally, food needs prior preparation before placing in a slow cooker, including chopping and some prior cooking. The same time temperature sanitation guidelines apply to slow cooking as they do to standard cooking.

Electric grills can add cooking options to the home cook's repertoire that they might not otherwise have. The one that everyone knows of is The George Foreman Grill®. At the height of their popularity, millions of units were sold on Home Marketing TV shows and in home supply stores throughout the world. Since then, others have copied the design so that now, there are many choices in design and function. Many of the standard units are marketed as Panini grills, although most open up so that the top and bottom surfaces are side by side, creating a wide open grilling surface. The Griddler® by Cuisinart is this type of unit with the additional feature of interchangeable surfaces so that the user can griddle (flat surface used for eggs and pancakes), grill (ridged surface used for grilling meat, fish, and vegetables), make waffles, or make panini.

Although it may not be in vogue, fried food is still a favorite among most Americans. If done properly, it does not have to be the grease soaked food that has given it a bad name. In the old days, Mom always used a pot of oil with a wire insert and cooked fried food on top of the stove. This method was not only a bit dangerous, but temperature control was always an issue. The easiest and safest way for the home cook to fry food on a regular basis is to do so in an **electric fryer**. The electric fryer has thermostatic control and no open flames to pose fire hazards. Use high temperature oil like peanut oil and strain the oil into an airtight container after each use, so that it can be used again. Discard oil after six months, if it exhibits excessive smoking when heated or has a rancid smell.

Quality **stand mixers** have become standard equipment for the modern kitchen. Kitchen Aid is by far the leader in this field. Some Kitchen Aid stand mixers are still in use after thirty-plus years of service. Not just for preparing dough and batter, the stand mixer affords the user a multitude of other functions by way of attachments. A short list of those attachments includes pasta roller and cutters, juicer, can opener, grater, grinder and sausage stuffer, and spiralizer. The connection for the attachments is universal in that they fit all sizes of mixers (5, 6, or 7 qt.) and have not been changed in the last fifty-plus years.

No modern kitchen would be complete without a **food processor**. Food processors have been used in professional kitchens for over fifty years and came into the home kitchen with the introduction of La Machine by Moulinex in the 1970s. The current standard bearer for home food processors is Cuisinart. Models come in a variety of sizes, from the handheld Mini Mate Plus 9 oz. to the 14-cup Elite. The standard size for most home kitchens is either the 8- or 11-cup model. All models come with the standard grinding blade, which can be used for most operations. Additional blades allow the user to slice, shred, and julienne with high accuracy and speed.

A **blender** is similar to a food processor with the following differences: blenders usually have less powerful motors that operate at higher RPMs; there are no interchangeable blades on a blender; the bowl of a blender is usually taller and of less volume than the bowl of a food processor. Blenders are best suited for preparing pureed drinks and crushing ice. The heavyweight champion of blenders is the Vitamix TurboBlend 4500. With a two-horsepower motor and 64-ounce polycarbonate bowl, the Vitamix may be used to prepare soups, dressings, sauces, baby food, and crushed ice, along with a host of other functions heretofore reserved for food processors.

Handheld blenders are a relatively new arrival in the home kitchen, although they have been in use in restaurants for many years. Handheld blenders (sometimes called "stick" blenders) are used to puree products without transferring to a bowl. Therefore, they are most suitable for pureeing a sauce on the stove or making a coulis in a heated pot. The advantage of a handheld blender is that the blender goes to the product. For conventional blenders, the product must always be transferred to the blender.

To summarize how to equip a start up kitchen, the following items are essential:

- Four burner range OR stand alone induction burner
- Self cleaning oven with convection option OR high capacity toaster oven with convection option
- Refrigerator/ freezer preferably under/over OR under counter refrigerator and freezer
- Microwave oven

Optional items that will make life in your kitchen easier are:

- 11-cup food processor
- Stand mixer
- Blender
- Immersion blender

- Rice cooker
- Slow cooker
- Electric grill
- Electric fryer

Cookware and Bakeware

Quality cookware is critical in achieving a level of consistency and variety in your culinary repertoire. Cookware should have two basic traits: conductivity and non-reactivity. Conductivity provides an evenly heated cooking surface, therefore reducing hot spots and subsequent burning. Non-reactivity provides unadulterated flavor and uncontaminated food products. There is, at this time, no single material that has both characteristics to a sufficient degree. Therefore, most manufacturers of high quality cookware incorporate at least two materials in multiple layers into a single piece.

The best conductors of heat are copper, aluminum, and cast iron. The most non-reactive materials are stainless steel and enamel. With the introduction of the Master Chef 2 line of cookware in 1971, All-Clad became the first cookware manufacturer to incorporate aluminum and stainless steel into one multiclad piece of cookware, thus starting a revolution in modern cookware. Other cookware manufacturers have since copied the design so that today, multiclad cookware is the state of the art in cooking. CIA Masters, Viking, and Sitram are a few of the manufacturers who incorporate both aluminum and copper with stainless steel into their cookware.

With the resurgence of induction cooktops in twenty-first century America, cookware manufacturers began to incorporate different alloys of stainless steel in the design to produce induction ready multiclad cookware. The only multiclad cookware that is induction ready has 18/0/0 stainless steel in the formula.

There are two categories of cookware, **pots and pans**. Pans are typically shorter and wider than pots and are used for sautéing and frying. A fry pan has perpendicular edges to contain the larger quantity of oil needed to fry. This pan is also called a *sautoir*. A sauté pan has beveled edges that allow steam to readily escape. This pan is also called a *sauteuse*.

It is somewhat confusing to purchase sauté and fry pans because nearly every manufacturer of cookware mislabels the two pans. This may sound like a bold statement, but further examination of the processes of frying and sautéing, for which the pans are named, should help to clarify this point.

Sautéing is a high heat minimal oil cooking method for medium to high quality food. It is important not to overload the pan because doing so will cool it down and the food will release water. Water is the enemy of sautéing. That's why a sauté pan has beveled edges to more readily allow the water to escape. An added feature of the design is that it allows the experienced practitioner to roll and flip the product.

Frying is a medium temperature oil immersion technique for cooking medium to high quality food. It is generally preferable and safer to fry in a thermostatically controlled electric fryolater. The stovetop process requires enough oil in the pan to float the product. This is typically an inch or so of oil. That's why the sides of a fry pan are perpendicular to the bottom so that the oil is contained in a safe manner.

If one needs further evidence of this nomenclature snafu; visit Anyrestaurant USA and go to the sauté station. You will probably find a stack of sauteuses and no sautoirs. Given the confusion on this issue, it may be better to describe a sauté pan as a beveled edge pan and a fry pan as a perpendicular edge pan when purchasing cookware.

No kitchen would be complete without at least one piece of **cast iron cookware**. Cast iron is one of the oldest continuously manufactured types of cookware in existence. Its manufacture and use in the US dates back more than one hundred years. One of the most unique properties of cast iron is its durability. It is possible that there are still some cast iron pans in use that are 100 years old. Cast iron is also very economical, not just because of its price point but also because it heats evenly and retains heat better than aluminum and stainless steel; therefore food can be prepared at lower temperatures. Lodge, the leading manufacturer of cast iron cookware recommends cooking at medium temperature for best results.

Properly seasoned cast iron creates its own nonstick surface. This surface improves with use. Some cast iron cookware is preseasoned at the factory. These pans are not fully seasoned and therefore require further seasoning before use. To complete the seasoning process, use the pan for frying or other types of cooking that require large amounts of oil. Do this a minimum of four times or until the surface of the pan turns smooth and dark black. Do not use the pan to cook food that is either high acid or high water until this process is complete. This would include tomato sauce and stew. Once the pan is thoroughly seasoned, the best way to keep it seasoned is to use it.

Sometimes cast iron pans lose their seasoning, either from non-use, abuse, or in the course of normal use. In these cases, it is necessary to re-season the pan. Use the following procedure to re-season:

- Wash, rinse and thoroughly dry the pan.
- Put one tablespoon of solid vegetable shortening or vegetable oil on a rag or use a pastry brush to rub a thin layer throughout the surface of the pan, inside and out (including the handle and lid if applicable.)
- Preheat the oven to 350° F and place the cookware upside-down in the oven with a drip pan on the lower level for three hours.
- Remove the pan from the oven and wipe clean with a paper towel.
- Repeat the process if necessary.

Like any other piece of cookware, removing all food particles, whether burned on or not, is a necessary procedure to maintain a sanitary cook surface. In all cases of cleaning cast iron, built up debris should not be confused with seasoning. Other than coated cast iron, there is no such thing as dishwasher safe cast iron cookware. Therefore, you should never clean cast iron cookware in the dishwasher. Don't allow soaking in the sink for any amount of time. Wash with a regular sponge; hot soapy water is fine. Dry immediately and apply a coating of oil for storage.

All kitchens should be stocked with at least one **nonstick fry pan** for cooking eggs. nonstick coatings came on the market after Dupont's invention of Teflon®, a polymer of ethylene and fluorine that has amazing nonstick properties. Once the patent expired, others manufactured the same material under the more generic PTFE (polytetrafluoroethylene). When applied to the surface of cookware, it imparts its nonstick properties to the pan, making it the perfect egg pan in years gone by.

After decades of production, PTFE coated cookware began to lose its appeal to the public due to several factors. Coatings were known to come off and end up in food if the pan was abused (heated at too high a temperature; used with abrasive tools). The conductivity of most pans left a lot to be desired; so that, even though food didn't stick, it burned. Finally, the last stake into the heart of PTFE coated cookware—health concerns. First, PTFE cookware that was overheated released vapors that were harmful to household pets. Some blamed the deaths of pet birds on the vapors. Then, the last strike—a health threat to humans. PFOA, a chemical used in the manufacture of PTFE, was found to pose a health risk to humans. Although the manufacturers argued that there were no traces of the chemical left in the product when applied to the cookware, it was to no avail. Sales of PTFE coated cookware plummeted and the cookware industry scrambled to find a substitute.

Out of that calamity, a new generation of nonstick cookware arose—ceramic titanium. Two manufacturers, Scan Pan and Swiss Diamond, soon led the pack. Ceramic titanium pans allow the user to cook at temperatures up to 500°F—much higher than PTFE coated pans—and the pans are dishwasher and metal utensil safe. The downside of these pans is that they are not induction ready. If you wish to use a nonstick pan on an induction burner, a Spanish company named Fagor manufactures such a product.

Some pans are used for baking and roasting. The **standard sheet pan** comes in three sizes: full, half, and quarter. A full sheet pan is used mostly in commercial applications. Due to its size (18" x 26"), it will not fit in most home ovens. The half sheet pan (13" x 18") and quarter sheet pan (9" x 13") are more suitable for home use. Sheet pans are used mostly for baking. However, the insertion of a rack will allow the user to roast on a sheet pan. Covering the sheet pan with a nonstick Silpat will prevent food from sticking and make cleanup easier.

Roasting pans are used for proper roasting in standard size ovens. Roasting pans should be made of thick conductive metal and contain a rack to elevate the roast from the bottom of the pan. All-Clad makes one of the best roasting pans with rack on the market.

Pots fall into two categories: **sauce pots and stock pots**. Sauce pots are generally smaller, with a single long handle. Sizes vary from 1 to 4 quarts. Stock pots are taller and larger than sauce pots and they have two short handles. They are usually 8–12 qt. capacity. A **Dutch oven** is a specific style of stock pot that is a bit squatter than a standard stock pot and they always have a lid. Dutch ovens are typically used on top of the stove and in the oven and are the preferred pot for camping. A typical Dutch oven is 8 qt capacity.

There are several types of cookware that fall outside the realm of traditional cookware that will enhance your cooking capacity. A **four piece multi-cooker** is one piece of cookware that all cooks with space challenged kitchens should have. The four pieces consist of a stock pot, usually 8–12 quarts; a colander-like pasta insert; a similar steamer insert; and a lid. A multi-cooker can be used to cook 2–3 items at the same time by using only one burner.

Pressure cooking at home has certainly come a long way from the days when the family had to evacuate the kitchen whenever mom made that corned beef in her old pressure cooker. Second generation pressure cookers, as all units made in the past four decades and marketed in the US must be, have taken the danger out of this quick and easy technique. Fagor is among the leaders in manufacturing quality pressure cookers at an affordable price. They offer an electric version that does not require a range burner for use and doubles as a rice cooker and slow cooker. Understanding how pressure cookers work can introduce the home cook to a safe cooking technique that will trim hours off your cooking time for stews, vegetables, and casseroles.

Pressure cookers work by taking a standard pot and designing it to incorporate a locking lid so that once heat is applied, the pressure inside the pot builds. At sea level, the atmospheric pressure is 14.7 pounds per square inch and the boiling point of water is 212°F. Since the pressure cooker is equipped with a locking lid, the pressure in the cooker is increased to 15 pounds above normal sea level pressure. The result is that the boiling point of water increases to 250°F inside the cooker.

The advantages of cooking at this higher than standard boiling point temperature is that foods cook in one third of the time. The steam pressure softens the fibers in food, tenderizing even tough meat in minutes. Foods become quickly infused with intense flavor because of the force of the steam. Foods with long cooking times like nutrient rich legumes are ready to eat in minutes, instead of hours. Fresh vegetables retain their vitamins, colors, and flavors because of shorter cooking times and minimal use of water.

A **stovetop smoker**, such as the one manufactured by Camerons, can add a unique element to one's cooking repertoire. The four-piece unit uses about two tablespoons of wood chips whose particle size is similar to that of saw dust. The wood is placed in the main housing and covered by a protective metal plate. A rack is placed on top to hold and elevate the food being smoked. The lid slides on to contain the majority of the smoke within the unit. The pan is then heated from below to start the smoking process. Since it also generates heat, the food is cooked and smoked. The unit generates minimal residual smoke (not enough to trigger most smoke alarms) and is induction ready. Some of the items that are particularly suited for the stove top smoker are trout, corn, ribs, and peppers.

The more variety you have in cookware, the greater your capabilities will be in the kitchen.

The following items are the essentials for stocking your kitchen:

- Saucepots: one 1–2 qt. and one 3–4 qts.
- Stockpots: one Dutch oven and one 8–12 qt. standard stockpot or multi-cooker
- Sauté pans from seven to twelve inches; with one nonstick for eggs
- One cast iron frying pan
- One quarter-sheet pan
- One half-sheet pan with rack

Optional pots and pans that will enhance your cooking experience are:

- Lodge Stovetop Grill
- Fagor pressure cooker
- Camerons Stovetop Smoker
- All-Clad roasting pan with rack

Hand Tools

A reliable, well-maintained knife is the most valuable item in a chef's tool kit. Knives are used in preparing nearly every meal that is produced in a professional kitchen. There are numerous manufacturers and styles of knives; thus selecting a knife for home use can sometimes be confusing. The highest priority when purchasing a knife should be how the knife feels in your hand and how it performs the tasks you will need it for. Therefore, you should never purchase a knife without trying it out first.

There are two basic techniques for making knives: stamping and forging. **Stamped knives** are knives whose blade has been stamped out of a sheet of steel. The quality of a stamped knife is in the steel tempering and finishing process. There is no bolster on a stamped knife because the stamping is from a single thickness of steel. Generally speaking, stamped knives are lighter and cheaper.

Forged knives are formed by a hot forge process, which hammers the knife into the desired shape from a single piece of steel. They are heavier and thicker than stamped knives. The forging process is a multi-step procedure. With similar use and maintenance, forged knives tend to last longer than stamped knives.

There are many shapes and styles for knives, and the design impacts the use for each. A chef's knife, usually 6 to 10 inches long, with 8 inches being the most popular length, is the most versatile and valuable knife in a chef's tool kit. Chef's knives have a belly shape to the blade to promote rocking. A paring knife has a small, straight blade, 2–4 inches in length. It is used for coring, paring, and fine work, such as garnishing. A slicing or carving knife has a long, thin

and flexible blade, 8–12 inches long. There are two distinct styles of non-serrated slicers: blunt and pointed tip. A blunt tip carving knife is used for slicing boneless roasts while a pointed tip carving knife is used for slicing meat with bones. A boning knife blade is usually 6 inches long, pointed, very narrow, and inflexible. It is used to remove meat from bones. A filet knife is similar in shape to a boning knife but the blade is very flexible to follow fish bones. A serrated knife has a saw-like edge and is ideal for slicing bread, tomatoes, citrus fruits, or anything with a tough exterior and a soft interior.

A vegetable peeler is a modified knife that is used to peel or pare fruits and vegetables. Paring is the removal of skin, while peeling is the removal of rind. The invention of the vegetable peeler has diminished the utility of a paring knife. The OXO replaceable blade vegetable peeler is one of the more efficient peelers on the market. Once the blade dulls, it can be replaced. Serrated vegetable peelers can peel difficult vegetables like tomatoes.

The parts of a knife all have specific names and functions. The blade is the cutting surface of the knife. The three areas of the blade are the tip, used for decorative cutting; the middle, used for general slicing and chopping; and the heel, which is the strongest part of the blade and is used for heavy work. The actual cutting edge of the blade is a very thin, flexible piece of metal with tiny teeth called the feather. The feather is what is realigned during the honing process. The spine is the back of the knife blade. It is sometimes used to brace the knife with the hand not on the handle for more support or pressure. The bolster is a raised portion of the metal blade that is between the cutting edge and the handle. It is typically found only on forged knives, although some stamped knives have attached bolsters. The tang is the portion of the metal that extends into the handle. Full tang refers to a blade that is secured in the handle with rivets extending through, thereby exposing the edge of the tang. Enclosed tang is one that is completely covered by the handle. Handles vary according to full or enclosed tangs. A knife should have a sure, comfortable fit and feel like an extension of the user's hand.

It is not cutting through food that dulls a knife; it's the repeated impact of the cutting edge against a chopping block or board. When this impact occurs, the microscopic teeth on the feather of the knife start to curl and flatten, causing the blade to feel dull. That is why a steel must be used everyday that you use your knife. The steel will realign the curl. This is called honing. If you use the

steel on a regular basis, you will find you will not have to sharpen your knife as often. Sharpening is different than honing. To sharpen a knife properly, some of the metal must be removed. A sharpening stone removes the first level of molecules from the blade, exposing a new edge.

For the ultimate in quick, consistent vegetable cuts, a **mandoline** is the tool of the professional. Several varieties with various capacities are available in a range of prices. Mandolines usually contain surgical quality blades and therefore the user should always wear a Forschner cut glove when using one. Julienne, waffle cut, and standard slicing are among the capabilities of most mandolines.

In order to fully appreciate the capability of a mandoline, it is important to understand the impact that design has on function. Since mandolines are used for the same purpose as are knives, a discussion of how each works is in order. In the case of a knife, the product is held stationary and the blade of the knife is moved in order to cut the food. In the case of the mandoline, the blade is stationary and the food is moved in order to cut it. The two basic motions when using a knife are slice and chop. In the case of a slice, the edge of the blade is moved horizontally across the surface of the food; in the case of a chop, the blade is repeatedly pressed down directly into the food. A combination of the two is sometimes used to chop.

Using this knowledge, one can predict the capabilities of a mandoline, based on the design, specifically taking into account the orientation of the blade with respect to the food. In the case of the V-slicer or other slicing mandolines where the blade is situated on an angle with respect to the food, the net effect is that the food is drawn across the blade in a manner that is similar to the slicing function of a knife. This is why these types of mandolines are more efficient for slicing. In the case of standard mandolines, the blade is oriented so that the food is introduced to the blade directly, which is similar to the chopping function of a knife. This is why these types of mandolines are generally incapable of slicing problem vegetables, such as a tomato or an eggplant that you wish to slice lengthwise. However, these types of mandolines generally offer more versatility.

Simpler versions of mandolines are used for specific cuts. The Börner julienne slicer is a cheap and simple way to make julienne cuts of potatoes, zucchini, carrots, and other vegetables. There is also a unit from the same company that produces wavy cuts. Both Progressive and Kyocera make a simple handheld

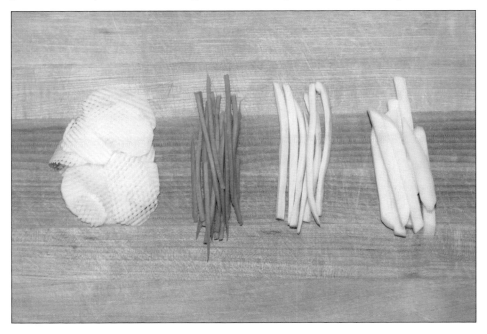

slicer that is capable of slicing the problem vegetables mentioned above. The V-Slicer is the original mandoline for home use and can be used to slice a variety of vegetables, including the aforementioned problem vegetables. In all of these cases, the drawback of each is that they are designed to perform a specific function and therefore generally produce a single cut.

There are many more complex mandolines available for use in the kitchen. Bron, a French company that has been manufacturing mandolines since their inception, is the standard mandoline for restaurant use. It is made entirely of metal and therefore has a longer life expectancy. The blade settings are somewhat difficult to change, making it more suitable for repetitive functions, as the setting is less susceptible to change during use; hence, the restaurant application. This is conversely why this particular mandoline may not be the best selection for home use. Other similar mandolines are made by Matfer and OXO. In all case, these mandolines are capable of performing the following cuts: straight slice and wavy slice of varying thickness (with the exception of the problem cuts), julienne, battonet and/or allumette, and waffle cut.

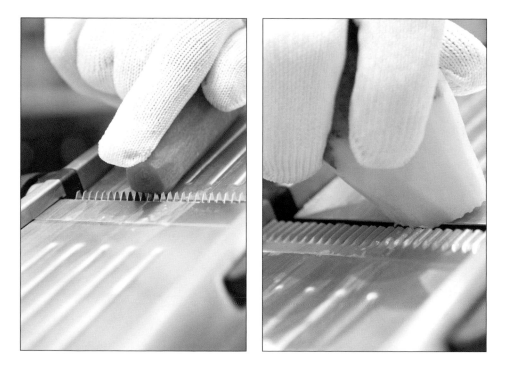

The OXO Steel Mandoline Slicer is the one exception to the standard mandoline's inability to slice the problem vegetables. It is made largely of steel and comes with two reversible blades. The first blade does the standard crinkle cut and a larger version of the same cut called ruffle cut. The second blade has the standard slicing edge that is used for variable straight slice. The reverse blade is what separates this mandoline from the others because this blade is serrated. The serration allows the user to slice eggplants longitudinally and slice tomatoes.

One of the other advantages of the OXO mandoline is that the julienne and battonet blades have a preset depth to them. On standard mandolines, when these two blades are engaged, the user must also set the depth of the cut in a trial and error manner, sometimes producing waste. On both OXO mandolines, this depth is set when the two blades are engaged, producing product from the start.

To summarize, the following items comprise a startup cutlery kit:

- Wooden or soft plastic cutting board
- Mineral oil if using wood cutting boards
- Honing steel
- 8" Chef knife
- 8–10" Pointed carving knife
- 3–4" Paring Knife
- Serrated bread knife
- Vegetable peeler

Optional items to add to your kit are:

- Non-flexible boning knife
- Flexible filet knife
- 7" Santoku knife
- 12" Blunt end carving knife
- Mandoline

Cutting Boards

Two types of cutting boards are recommended for use with high quality knives in order to preserve their edge and lengthen their life. The classic cutting board is made of hardwood, such as maple. Hardwood, when properly maintained, is non-absorbent and is resistant to nicking and scratching. It is also "knife friendly" in that it yields slightly when contacted with the cutting edge of a knife. Non-absorbent, high-density polypropylene and polyethylene cutting boards have similar properties. Never use your knife on a hard surface such as marble, glass, or stainless steel. These hard surfaces will curl the microscopic cutting edge of the knife, ruining the blade.

Both wooden and plastic cutting boards require proper care and maintenance in order to extend their life and guard against food borne illness. In order to avoid cross-contamination of potentially hazardous food, it is recommended that boards be dedicated to a single food product, e.g., one board for vegetables and one board for meat. Some boards have color-coded sides to denote their use. Cutting boards should be cleaned and sanitized between each use. Plastic boards may be cleaned and sanitized in a properly maintained high-temperature or chemical sanitizing dishwasher. Alternatively, they may be washed in hot, soapy water to remove food particles, rinsed with hot water, and immersed in a 100 ppm chlorine solution for one minute. This solution may be prepared by dissolving one tablespoon of household bleach in one gallon of water. Always air-dry a cutting board to maintain a sanitary surface.

Wooden cutting boards should never be used immediately upon purchasing. They should first be treated with mineral oil in order to establish a barrier against absorption. Use only mineral oil and not vegetable oils or animal fat to treat the board. Apply a coating of oil with a clean towel and wipe off any excess. Repeat the process the following day. Begin using the board on the third day. Between uses, clean the board with a mild soap solution and a non-abrasive sponge to remove food particles. Rinse thoroughly. Sanitize by spraying with a 100 ppm chlorine solution. Air-dry after sanitizing. Apply another coat of mineral oil if the board appears to be drying out or the color is fading. Never clean a wooden cutting board in a dishwasher.

Thermometers

One gadget that all cooks should have in their tool kit is a reliable meat thermometer. Cooking meat via time charts or using forks to bleed the meat are unreliable methods of determining the degree of doneness. To protect yourself from food borne illness, always use a reliable meat thermometer to test for doneness. In order to choose a thermometer for home use, some of the qualities to look for are:

- **Accuracy:** accuracy is the ability to produce a reading that is close to the true value. It is usually expressed as a percentage of the reading or as a deviation from true. Precision is not the same as accuracy. Precision is the ability to produce readings that are close to each other. A thermometer with an accuracy of ± 2° is considered accurate enough for food service.
- **Resolution:** the ability to distinguish between the units of measurement. This is a measure of the readability of the gauge or display. It should be noted that resolution has no true effect on accuracy. A digital thermometer that reads out in tenths of a degree, for instance, has no more accuracy than one that reads out in whole numbers if they both have the same standard deviation.
- **Range:** the working range in degrees of the thermometer. It is better to purchase a thermometer with a narrow working range, if that range matches the one you are interested in. For instance, the temperature inside a refrigerator is better measured with a thermometer whose range is -20° to 60° as opposed to one with a range of -20° to 300°. The range has a direct effect on resolution and an indirect effect on accuracy.
- **Response Time:** the length of time it takes to obtain an accurate reading. Beware of advertising. Some manufacturers list response time for an initial reading as opposed to an accurate reading. In these cases, it usually takes five such readings to obtain an accurate reading.
- **Immersion Length:** the minimum and maximum depths that the probe must be inserted into the food to obtain an accurate reading. This is generally a function of construction. Shorter minimum immersion lengths allow the user to measure the temperature of smaller, thinner items, like hamburgers.
- **Ease of Operation:** some thermometers are worth their sale price because they provide a service other than temperature measurement. Probe thermometers whose readout may be positioned outside the oven allow the user to monitor the cooking process without opening the oven door. Similarly, thermometers with warning buzzers and timers provide a safety net against overcooking. Thermometers that read degrees of doneness for certain types of meat in addition to temperature do not require the user to remember the individual temperatures. It should be noted that these thermometers usually cook food to a higher temperature than is necessary.

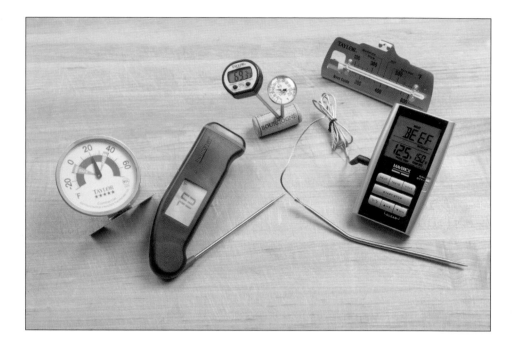

There are many types of thermometers on the market today. Some of the most common are:

- **Column of liquid:** the standard glass thermometer that is filled either with mercury or alcohol. For food service applications, the liquid would never be mercury. As the temperature rises, the liquid expands within the column and the temperature is read on the scale alongside. This is a very recognizable means of measuring temperature. They are particularly suited for continuous or nearly continuous applications, such as measuring the temperature of an oven, refrigerator or oil bath.
- **Bimetal:** works on the principle that two metals, when heated, will expand at different rates. Most dial thermometers are bimetal. They require frequent calibration and they have minimal accuracy. Some models offer larger dials for enhanced readability.
- **Thermistor:** a semi-conductor sandwiched between two pieces of epoxy. Most digital thermometers are of this type. They are more accurate than the bimetals, require little calibration, and have greater resolution. True response time is about thirty seconds.
- **Thermocouple:** works on the principle that certain metals emit a low-level DC voltage when heated. When two dissimilar metals are bound together, the instru-

ment measures the differential voltage and converts it directly to temperature. These are extremely accurate and operate over a wide range of temperatures. Unlike thermistors, thermocouples may be calibrated at two settings, providing accurate readings over the entire range. Response time is less than five seconds.

- **RTD:** Resistance Temperature Device. Operates on the principle that platinum has a very predictable and reproducible resistance to electric current at any given temperature. As the temperature changes, the resistance is measured in ohms and converted directly to temperature. This is the most accurate thermometer that is available in the food service industry. It requires no calibration and operates over a wide linear range. Given the cost of platinum, RTD thermometers tend to be quite expensive.
- **Infrared:** an optical detector used to measure surface temperatures only. It operates on the principle that any heated surface emits electromagnetic radiation in the infrared region. Generally used in the form of a gun that is pointed at the surface from a short distance. Usually equipped with LASER sighting.

In the case of meat thermometers, two basic varieties are in use today. A bimetal thermometer is the standard dial thermometer that has been used for generations. The temperature is easy to read and the thermometer often has temperatures for cooking meats displayed on the dial. Bimetal thermometers require occasional calibration, particularly after any sort of thermal or percussive shock, such as being left in an oven or dropped on a hard floor. The readings are usually to the nearest degree and the insertion length for reliable readings is usually two to three inches.

Digital thermometers offer a more convenient way of measuring meat temperatures. Digital thermometers read out in tenths of a degree, require no calibration and have insertion lengths of one to two inches. Digital thermometers require a small battery to operate. Taylor, the leader in that field, makes both thermometers, although the current "Cadillac of Thermometers" is undoubtedly the Thermapen.

Whisk

A **whisk** is a well-balanced kitchen utensil composed of uniformly shaped wires that curve into a handle, and when used to whip, efficiently incorporates air into food. Whisks are available in many shapes and sizes depending on the task at hand. The number of wires ranges from two to twenty. Additionally, the wires' thicknesses and shapes coupled with their material make-up affect how the air is incorporated into the mixture. The wires may be made of stainless

steel, nylon, wood, and even rattan. Handles are composed of stainless steel, wood, or nylon to aid in comfort as well as utility (i.e., heat resistance).

The **standard or sauce whisk** (sometimes called a French whisk) has approximately nine rigid wires looped into a pear shape. This aids in mixing, emulsifying, and aerating. Its thick wires make it a good choice to work with heavy mixtures. The nine wires increase the per-stroke capability. Sauce whisks range in size from 8–18 inches. A wooden handle is a good choice for a sauce whisk because it is often immersed in a hot pot for extended periods of time and the wooden handle is more heat resistant than other materials. This whisk is perfect for whipping eggs or blending sauces and dressings.

A **Balloon whisk** is the optimum whisk for whipping air into cream or egg whites. Its bulb shape and pliant wires increase the area of contact with the mixture, thereby speeding up the process. The best balloon whisks have thin rather than thick wires, and will not push out air already incorporated. Balloon whisks with a ball inside are used to incorporate more air into the product. The ball tends to keep product from becoming trapped inside the whisk.

The **flat whisk** is perfect for incorporating flour into melted butter and in preparing roux based sauces. The four or five wires lie flat, creating a larger area to work with. The slight upward bow of the wires offsets the handle, providing a more comfortable fit and easier access to the bottom edge of the saucepan. This whisk also works well for beating eggs in a shallow bowl.

Coiled whisks are a tool for mixing & aerating small amounts of thin batter. Its advantage is that each coil is in contact with the pan's surface (bottom & sides of pan). They should not be used with thick sauces or batters because they clog easily. To use a coiled whisk, hold the handle between both hands and move your hands back and forth to rotate the coils at a rapid rate.

Spatulas

Spatulas are among the most diverse tools in the kitchen. There are many varieties, each with specific uses. **Plastic or rubber spatulas** are used mostly in baking, to remove batters and doughs from bowls. A similar tool, called a **bowl scraper** is essentially a rubber spatula without a handle. Both tools are used extensively in restaurants to minimize food loss during transfer from one vessel to another.

There are several types of metal spatulas. The most common is a narrow flat piece of stainless steel with a handle, similar in shape to a knife. It is also referred to as a **palette knife.** It is primarily used to remove cakes from pans and also to ice cakes. An **offset cake spatula** is very similar to a palette knife but the handle is offset to the blade; that is, the handle is not in a straight line with the blade. They are used primarily for cake decorating so that the user's hand does not contact the cake while icing. A **grill spatula** is a wide offset metal spatula that is used to manipulate and remove items from a grill. One variety is perforated (with holes on the contact surface) in order to remove food and leave fat or oil behind. A **fish spatula** has a slotted surface and a slanted blade. It is used to remove and manipulate fish on a grill. It is slotted to separate the oil from the fish and slanted to protect the delicate flesh of the fish.

Strainers, Colanders

In many cases, food must be separated from the liquid that surrounds it, either cooking or rinsing liquid. There are generally two tools that accomplish this task: **a strainer and a colander.** Colanders are made of metal or plastic in the shape of a bowl with a series of holes so that the liquid flows through and the product is contained within. Strainers are usually smaller than colanders. They have a bowl shaped body constructed of wire mesh which is attached to a handle. They are used to separate liquid from smaller particle food, as the holes in the mesh are much smaller than those of colander.

There are two other strainer/colanders that are used mainly in commercial kitchens; however, home cooks can raise their game by using them. A **China cap** is a modified colander with a conical shape. **A chinois** is a modified strainer with the same shape as a China cap. Unlike the strainer or colander, in most instances, the desired product is passed through the two leaving the undesired material behind. Just as in the case of the strainer and colander, the material that passes through a chinois is much finer than the product that passes through a China cap.

Spoons

Spoons are used to stir, transfer, and serve food. They are usually made of wood, metal, or plastic; although silicone spoons have become popular because of their inertness and ability to withstand high temperatures. Wooden spoons are most often used for stirring the contents of a pot because they do not conduct heat and will not scratch the interior of the pot. Metal and plastic spoons come in three styles: **non-perforated, perforated, and slotted**. Silicone spoons tend to follow the same construction.

Tongs are a form of modified spoons that are used to lift solid objects from pans or other vessels and either manipulate them within the pan or transfer them to another location. Some tongs have plastic coatings on the service end so that they can be used with nonstick cookware.

Bowls

Bowls are used for mixing, folding, and serving food. They can be made of metal, glass or wood. Wooden bowls are used mostly for serving salad. Metal bowls are used mainly in baking for making dough and batter. Glass bowls are used for holding raw materials prior to cooking. In this utility, they are often referred to as *mise en place* bowls. (More on that term in Chapter 10.)

Baking

Baking is a more precise science than cooking at large. When preparing an entrée, appetizer, or other dish, one has the option of sampling midway through the preparation or just before serving and adjusting the seasoning and consistency as needed. The process of baking, however, does not allow for this luxury. Unlike cooking at large, the composition of baked goods needs to be accurately set before it is baked. Therefore, it is imperative that bakers and pastry chefs follow a tested recipe in order to achieve consistent quality in the end product. This requires accurate measurement of the starting materials and accordingly reliable measuring devices.

There are two ways to measure ingredients in cooking or baking. The most common method of accurately measuring the ingredients in home baking is by volume. The typical units of measurement are teaspoons (t.), tablespoons (T.), fluid ounces (fl. oz.), cups (c.), quarts (qt.), gallons (gal.) and fractions thereof. The devices used to measure these specific volumes bear the same names as the units. These devices are of distinctly different design when measuring solids versus liquids. The units themselves are identical. However, the different constructions for solid and liquid measuring devices are designed for accurate measuring and dispensing of each.

All volumetric measuring devices have two listed capacities that are specific to each. The working capacity is the largest volume that can be accurately measured and dispensed. The nominal capacity is the largest volume that the container will hold regardless of accuracy or measurement. Therein lies the difference between a solid, or dry measure and a liquid measure. The nominal capacity and working capacity of a dry measure are the same. The nominal capacity of a liquid measure is greater than the working capacity of the same measure. These properties are evident in the design and use of each.

Using a standard measuring cup as the example, a dry measuring cup is specific to each individual unit being measured; i.e., a half-cup measure is used only to measure a half cup of an ingredient; ¼-cup measure is used exclusively to measure ¼ cup, etc. As such, the solid, usually granular or a powder, is placed in the cup to extend above the rim. It is then leveled off to the nominal capacity of the cup by using a spatula or palette knife so that what is left in the cup is exactly what the size of the cup is; therefore, an accurate dry measure.

If the same cup design were used to measure and dispense a liquid, it would present at least two problems. The first problem would be in accurately measuring the liquid. Since the liquid would need to be poured to a level exactly equal to the nominal capacity of the cup, it would almost certainly be a bit less or spill over. The second problem would be accurately dispensing the liquid without spilling it. That is why a liquid measure always contains a spout and the delineations that determine each volume stop short of the rim of the cup. This is also why a liquid measure can be used to dispense a variety of volumes.

When choosing a set of measuring spoons, it is better to purchase a set with the size engraved in the spoon, such as in the case of metal spoons. When the delineation is written or stamped on a measuring spoon, they tend to become erased over time through continuous use and contact.

Dishers

Dishers are valuable tools for measuring and discharging repetitious amounts of food. Most home cooks might identify a disher as an ice cream scoop. The design of a scoop is quite different, however than that of a disher. A scoop is used in flour and sugar bins and ice machines in restaurants to dispense those products. Scoops look a bit like shovels whose sides have been beveled to form a cup.

Dishers are particularly valuable because there is an internationally recognized system for identifying each disher and the exact volume that it dispenses. The numbering system lists the number of times one would need to measure and dispense water using that particular disher in order to end up with a total volume of one quart. Therefore, the higher the number of the disher, the smaller the volume it dispenses. That number is usually stamped on the inside of the handle. Dishers are most frequently used in making cookies and meatballs. However, they are used extensively in commercial cooking to dispense a variety of products quickly.

Ricer and Mill

Other gadgets that will allow the home cook to prepare quick, tasty meals include a potato ricer and a food mill. A potato ricer is used to process boiled potatoes into mashed or Duchess potatoes. After being pressed through the ricer, or "riced," the potatoes can be converted to mashed potatoes by adding the remaining ingredients and stirring with a wooden spoon. This is a technique that is superior to whipping with a mixer in that the particle size is more uniform and the potatoes are processed for less time. Sometimes potatoes that are whipped on a handheld or stand mixer become gummy because the method places too much torque on the product. The net effect is that this excessive torque shatters the cell walls of the potato, releasing starch and causing the product to become gummy. A food mill is primarily used to process fruits and vegetables for use in sauces and coulis. The food is both ground and strained; yielding a product that is of uniform size and eliminating any undesired parts of the starting material, such as berry seeds.

Additional Tools

Additional tools that might be helpful to have on hand when cooking include a bench scraper, a zester, and a pastry brush. A **bench scraper** is a flat piece of metal that has a rubber, plastic, or wooden guard on the end that is held in the hand. They are usually 6" by 3" with the long side being the working side. They are used to safely and accurately move food from one surface to another. They are especially valuable in manipulating dough when rolling out.

Zesters come in two varieties. They are used to remove the outer part of the rind from citrus fruits. This part, called the **zest**, contains a higher percentage of the essential oils that give each fruit their distinct flavor. Therefore; zest is often used in recipes to impart that flavor to the dish. The classic zester is a small handheld tool that produces thin, long pieces of zest. Some of them are also **channel knives**, which produce wider pieces of zest.

The microplane zester was invented by a carpenter's wife and its design resembles that of a chisel. It produces much finer zest than the classic channel knife and is therefore suited to recipes where the zest will not be removed from the final product. It is also suitable for grating nutmeg and cheese.

Pastry brushes are used to evenly coat surfaces with liquids. In baking, that liquid is often melted butter, egg wash, or fruit glazes. They may also be used to apply marinades and sauces to savory food. A classic pastry brush looks like a small paint brush. The bristles are made of fiber. Therefore it can not be used for high temperature applications, like spreading barbecue sauce on a piece of meat while it is on the grill. For those applications, silicone pastry brushes can get the job done without burning the bristles.

To summarize, the following tools are essential for stocking a startup kitchen:

- Meat thermometer, preferably Thermapen
- Balloon whisk
- French whisk
- 8" Offset perforated grill spatula
- Rubber spatula
- Colander
- Strainer
- Wooden spoon
- Perforated metal spoon
- Non-perforated metal spoon
- 8–12" tongs
- Wooden salad bowl
- Glass bowls
- Metal bowls
- 2-cup liquid measure
- Set of dry measure cups
- Set of measuring spoons
- #100 Disher
- #50 Disher
- #12 Disher
- Bench scraper

Optional tools that will make your cooking experience more enjoyable include:

- Potato ricer
- Food mill
- Microplane zester
- Standard zester with channel knife
- Chinois
- China cap
- Standard pastry brush
- Silicone pastry brush
- Fish spatula
- Flat whisk
- Slotted spoon
- 2-qt. Liquid measure

CHAPTER THREE

Fruits, Vegetables, and Grains

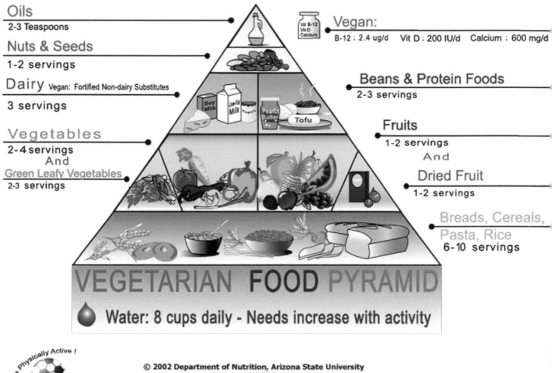

Oils
2-3 Teaspoons

Nuts & Seeds
1-2 servings

Dairy Vegan: Fortified Non-dairy Substitutes
3 servings

Vegetables
2-4 servings
And
Green Leafy Vegetables
2-3 servings

Vit B-12 Vit D Calcium

Vegan:
B-12 : 2.4 ug/d   Vit D : 200 IU/d   Calcium : 600 mg/d

Beans & Protein Foods
2-3 servings

Fruits
1-2 servings
And
Dried Fruit
1-2 servings

Breads, Cereals, Pasta, Rice
6-10 servings

Soy Milk   Milk   Peanut Butter   Tofu

VEGETARIAN FOOD PYRAMID

Water: 8 cups daily - Needs increase with activity

Be Physically Active !

© 2002 Department of Nutrition, Arizona State University
Art by Nick Rickert

Beyond reading food labels and understanding some of the terminology used to describe food, the informed shopper should know a bit about the major categories of food, such as vegetables, starches, fruit, meat, poultry, seafood, and dairy. The following passages should help to serve as a guide for this purpose.

VEGETABLES

Corn

Corn is one of the most versatile and prolific cereal grains in the world. It is of the genus and species *Zea mays* and was first cultivated in Mexico and Central America. By the time of Columbus's arrival in the New World, corn was being cultivated by most of the indigenous people of North America. It was traded to the early settlers, who gave it the name "Indian Corn." Europeans call it maize, after the Indian word *mahiz*. Virtually every part of the plant has some utility. The husks can be used to wrap tamales, the silk to make tea, the stalks as cattle fodder and the grain as a staple for humans and livestock. Hominy is the dried kernel from which the hull and germ have been removed. It is most often ground into grits, a breakfast mainstay in the Southern United States.

Farmers generally place corn into two categories: feed corn, sometimes called field or dent corn, and sweet corn. The latter is the type you would find in the grocery store or farmer's market. Horticulturists have developed the two major varieties used today. They are white corn, called Country Gentleman and yellow, or Golden Bantam corn. A hybrid known as butter and sugar corn produces ears that have both yellow and white kernels. Sweet corn is also categorized according to sugar content. The sweetest is called super-sweet; the least sweet is called standard or heirloom. Sugar-enhanced corn has a sweetness somewhere between the other two.

The key to cooking the sweetest and therefore the best corn is quite simple- the quicker the process from stalk to stockpot, the better the quality. For best results, corn should be picked and cooked immediately. This is because as soon as it is picked, corn begins the process that converts the sugar to starch, thereby losing some of its sweetness and flavor. If you don't grow your own corn, you should purchase corn from a farmer or farmer's market. In selecting corn, choose ears whose silk is pale and slightly sticky with brownish tips. The cut should be fresh, moist, and free of spots. The kernels should fill the entire ear and should release a milky juice if squeezed. Cook the corn in lots of boiling, unsalted water, about a gallon for four ears. There is no need to add sugar to the water if the corn is fresh. **Never overcook corn**. Five minutes in the pot should be enough time to cook corn.

Squash

Squashes are members of the gourd family, which also includes cucumbers and pumpkins. They are native to both the New World and Old World. Evidence of squash being eaten in Mexico dates back to 5500 BC. The word squash comes from the American Indian word *askutasquash*. With the exception of cucumbers and pumpkins, squashes are divided into summer and winter varieties. Summer squash have thin, edible skins and soft seeds. They are harvested before reaching maturity. Locally grown summer squash is best harvested from early to late summer. They are very perishable and should be prepared within 5 days of harvest. Due to their high water content, they generally cook quickly. Frying and sautéing are the preferred cooking techniques, although they may also be baked or steamed. The flowers are edible and in some cultures they are batter dipped and fried or sautéed in addition to being stuffed and baked.

In recent years, the selection of summer squash varieties has increased as new disease-resistant hybrids have been introduced. The three basic fruit shapes and colors are: scallop or pattypan (round or flat with scalloped edges, usually white, yellow or green); constricted neck (thinner at the stem end than the blossom end and classified as crookneck or straightneck); cylindrical to club-shaped Italian marrows (zucchini, cocozelle and caserta; usually shades of green, but also yellow or white). Scallop varieties include white bush scallop (pattypan), Peter Pan, scaloppini and sunburst. Constricted neck varieties include early yellow summer crookneck, sundance, early prolific straightneck and goldbar. Italian marrow varieties include black zucchini, black beauty, cocozelle, vegetable marrow, white bush, aristocrat, chefini, classic, elite, embassy, president, spineless beauty, and goldrush. Other hybrids include butter blossom, gourmet globe, and sun drops. Marrow squash is a zucchini that is harvested when mature and is therefore very large. They are popular in England where they are usually stuffed and baked or made into jam. Chayotes, also called christophene or mirliton, are grown in the Southern US and throughout Latin America. Summer squash are high in vitamins A and C and niacin.

Tomatoes

All species of tomatoes are of the genus *Lycopersicon*, from the *Solanaceae* family. The genetic roots of the wild species are almost certainly in the Western coast of South America, from Peru to Northern Chile, including the Galapagos Islands. Several thousand years ago, the wild species made its way from Peru to Central America, where the Aztecs began to cultivate it. By the time Cortez arrived in 1521, the Aztecs were consuming a dish comprised of tomatoes, peppers, and salt (the first salsa?). The tomato was subsequently brought to Spain.

The tomato began to gain acceptance in the American diet in the nineteenth century. In 1835, they were sold in Boston's Quincy Market. In 1847, Thomas Bridgeman listed four varieties in his seed catalog. With the emergence of new cultivars, the physiology of the tomato began to change. Wild tomatoes were small, about the size of a cherry tomato, with tough skins. The new cultivars were larger, with thin, red skins. The first hybrid was the Mikado, introduced by Rice's Seed Company in 1880. The appeal of this and future hybrids was increased size, resistance to disease and decreased acidity. Hybrids have since become the dominant cultivars in America.

The main drawback with hybrids, as many home gardeners will tell you, is that the seeds must be purchased each year from the seed manufacturer. If the seeds from the previous year's crops are planted, many variations, including undesirable product will result. To take matters into their own hands, and also to sample some of the classic tomatoes of yesteryear, many home gardeners are opting to plant heirloom tomatoes. With colorful names and stories to match, heirlooms like Mortgage Lifter and Jeff Davis have lineages that are unchanged for the last 100 years or more. Most are distinct in color, shape, and size. The drawbacks to heirlooms are decreased yield and low resistance to disease.

The status of the tomato in the US has evolved over time from that of a poisonous ornamental berry to a major source of nutrition. It is ranked sixteenth among all fruits and vegetables as a source of vitamin A and thirteenth in vitamin C. When corrected for per capita consumption, the tomato is the number one source of these two nutrients in the American diet. Recent studies indicating that lycopene, a carotenoid found in high concentrations in tomatoes, may be a potent anti-oxidant with connections to cancer prevention, have further elevated the status of the tomato to that of health food. The US is also the number one tomato producer in the world.

Peppers

Hot peppers, or chilies find their way into a myriad of flavorful dishes and cuisines, from Asian to Latin to Regional American. The chemical that gives spicy peppers their heat is *capsaicin* or capsicum. It is found in various levels depending on the particular type of pepper. The higher the capsicum level, the hotter the pepper will be.

The **Scoville Scale**, created by Wilbur Scoville in 1912, is a measure of the capsaicin level and therefore spiciness of various peppers. The original procedure for determining this value was an organoleptic, or taste, test. A solution of the pepper extract was diluted with a sugar solution until a panel of five tasters determined it was no longer hot. This method, while still in use in most food manufacturing facilities has been replaced by more precise analytical techniques. High Performance Liquid Chromatography (HPLC) is able to separate and quantify each of the various compounds that contribute to the spiciness of peppers. These values are then converted to Scoville Units for uniformity. A concentration of one part per-million capsaicin is equivalent to 15 Scoville Units.

Potatoes

Potatoes are indigenous to South America and were introduced to the rest of the world 400 to 500 years ago. Since then, they have become an important food source for much of the world's population. They are the fourth most cultivated crop in the world. A member of the nightshade family, potatoes are not a root vegetable but rather a tuber, which is a modified stem, often formed underground where energy is stored. This function accounts for the high starch level of potatoes.

There are over four thousand varieties of potatoes grown today. The most visible types are: russet, which have brown skin and are elongated and therefore easy to peel and process; red skin, sometimes referred to as "new potatoes," no peeling required making them excellent boiling potatoes; Yukon Gold, which are prized for their color and flavor; and fingerling, a current favorite in restaurants.

THE SCOVILLE SCALE

Scoville Units	Pepper / Item
2,200,000	Carolina Reaper
2,009,231	Trinidad Moruga Scorpion
1,900,000	7 Pot Brain Strain
1,900,000	7 Pot Primo
1,853,936	7 Pod Douglah (7 Pod Douglah; Chocolate 7 Pot; 7 Pot Brown)
1,463,700	Butch T. Trinidad Scorpion
1,359,000	Naga Viper
1.0–1.3 Million	Trinidad 7 Pot Jonah
1,041,427	Bhut Jolokia
1,000,000	Naga Morich
876,000–970,000	Dorset Naga(British)
800,000	Trinidad Yellow 7 Pot
350,000–580,000	Red Savina Habanero
100,000–350,000	Habanero Chile
100,000–325,000	Scotch Bonnet
100,000–225,000	African Birdseye
100,000–200,000	Jamaican Hot Pepper
100,000–125,000	Carolina Cayenne Pepper
95,000–110,000	Bahamian Pepper
85,000–115,000	Tabiche Pepper
50,000–100,000	Chiltepin Pepper
50,000–100,000	Rocoto
40,000–58,000	Pequin Pepper
40,000–50,000	Super Chile Pepper
40,000–50,000	Santaka Pepper
30,000–50,000	Cayenne Pepper
30,000–50,000	Tabasco Pepper
15,000–30,000	De Arbol Pepper
12,000–30,000	Manzano Pepper
5,000–23,000	Serrano Pepper
5,000–10,000	Hot Wax Pepper
5,000–10,000	Chipotle
2,500–8,000	Jalapeno
2,500–5,000	Guajilla Pepper
2,500	Tabasco Sauce
1,500–2,500	Rocotilla Pepper
1,000–2,000	Pasilla Pepper
1,000–2,000	Ancho Pepper
1,000–2,000	Poblano Pepper
700–1,000	Coronado Pepper
500–2,500	Anaheim Pepper
500–1,000	New Mexico Pepper
500–700	Santa Fe Grande Pepper
100–500	Pepperoncini Pepper
100–500	Pimiento
0	Bell Pepper

Potatoes can be stored under controlled temperatures for up to ten months. However; the conditions that will allow for this long shelf life are not readily available in the home kitchen. The perfect storing temperature is 39° to 50° F and they should be stored in a well ventilated area. In days gone by, this would be done in a cold cellar. Subjecting potatoes to temperatures below 39° causes the starch to convert to sugar, impacting the flavor. That's why potatoes should not be stored in a refrigerator. They should be stored in a hanging basket in a cool part of the house. Since the temperature in most homes is not in the optimum range for storing potatoes, the shelf life of potatoes stored in hanging baskets is approximately 2–3 weeks.

Potatoes are quite versatile in cooking. They can be boiled, roasted, fried, or baked. The type of potato used for each is determined by the type of starch in the potato. Floury, or mealy potatoes are called baking potatoes. They have a higher starch level than waxy, or boiling potatoes. Russets are baking potatoes and red potatoes are boiling potatoes; although many cooks use both varieties for boiling or baking.

Leaf Vegetables

Leaf vegetables are an important part of a balanced diet and should be consumed daily. They are sometimes referred to as pot herbs, greens, or salad greens. Many varieties can be consumed raw, hence the name salad greens. They are typically quick growing and can produce multiple harvests during a single growing season. Because they are leaves and therefore are responsible for photosynthesis, they are very high in Vitamin K. They are also a valuable source of fiber, Vitamin A, and Vitamin C. Common varieties include spinach, chard, lettuces, and turnip greens.

Greens may be boiled, sautéed, stir fried, stewed, or steamed. Typically they lose considerable volume upon cooking. In the Southern US in particular, various greens, like collards, mustard greens, and turnip greens are cooked with pork products and are considered to be soul food.

Spinach is a member of the amarynth family, originating in Persia. Spinach is very high in Iron and B vitamins, making it one of the healthiest of all greens to eat. US consumption of spinach soared after the creation of baby spinach and the triple washing procedure that made it much easier to use. Prior to that, standard leaf spinach was typically loaded with dirt and sand and required meticulous multiple wash and rinse prior to consumption.

Spinach can be served either raw or cooked. No restaurant menu would be complete without a spinach salad on the menu. While some boil spinach to cook it, the most common manner of preparation in use today is direct cooking in a sauté pan with minimal oil or butter. The rendered water of the spinach itself cooks the product. Spinach is popular outside the US in dishes like the Indian *Saag Paneer*, where it is stewed with ginger and sometimes chilies and then served with fried cheese on top.

There are many varieties of **lettuce** on the market today. Lettuce is typically eaten in salads in the US. In France, certain lettuces are sliced thinly and used to finish soup. Iceberg lettuce is very popular in the US, mostly due to its ease of processing and crispy texture. While not as nutritionally valuable as some of the leafier varieties of lettuce, it is a ubiquitous offering on steak house menus in the form of a wedge salad. Boston lettuce, sometimes referred to as bib lettuce, has a velvety soft texture that, when mixed with other types of lettuce gives a salad a broader texture profile. Heads are very small, making them a bit costly. Red leaf and green leaf lettuces are the go-to variety for salad in many restaurants. Their broad leaves make them easy to clean and the contrast in color make them visually stimulating when mixed together.

Microgreens come in many forms and have grown in popularity over the past twenty years. **Frisee, mâche, Lola Rossa,** and **oak leaf** are varieties that can be found in some of the packaged salad mixes. They are in particularly wide use in restaurants as they are valued for their taste, texture and visual appeal.

Root Vegetables

Root vegetables are a valuable source of vitamins and minerals in the American diet. Because they grow underground, they also have the advantage of being able to withstand colder climates and therefore, they are generally available year round. Many root vegetables, like carrots and beets, are also high in carbohydrates.

Carrots originate in their wild form from Persia. Since cultivation, farmers have selectively bred carrots to have larger, less woody and sweeter tap roots, which is the portion of the plant that most would identify as a carrot. Typically bright orange, carrots may also be black, white, purple, red, yellow or combinations thereof. Approximately half the world's harvest currently comes from China.

Carrots are very high in beta-carotene and other carotenoids. These compounds are easily metabolized into Vitamin A. A 4-ounce potion of carrots provides 100 percent of the RDA for Vitamin A. Carrots are also high in Vitamins K and B6. A typical orange carrot is about 5 percent sugar.

Carrots may be consumed raw, either in convenient, easy to transport sticks or shredded in a salad. In stick form, they are a healthy snack food or an essential member of a crudite. Carrots can be boiled, stir fried, or roasted. When they are boiled, they are often glazed in butter and brown sugar afterward. When stir fried, carrots are usually shredded first, as they tend to take longer to cook than other stir fry vegetables. Roasting brings out all the sugar in carrots by way of caramelizing.

Turnips are members of the brassica family, which includes cabbage, cauliflower, broccoli, and Brussels sprouts.. They have been cultivated for about 3500 years, often in cold climate areas. When cultivated mostly for the root, they are referred to as white turnips. When cultivated for the leaves, they are referred to as Chinese cabbage. Both leaves and root are edible and both have a bitter taste. They are very popular in the southern US, where leaves and root are combined and boiled, often with pork product.

Broccoli rabe, rappini, and Chinese broccoli are all members of the turnip, and therefore, brassica family. The leaves contain high levels of Vitamins C, K, and A while the root is also a good source of Vitamin C. Leaves of most varieties of turnips are mostly steamed or boiled. Turnip roots are mostly boiled and often served mashed. **Rutabagas,** often called yellow turnips are large and waxy and have a similar bitter flavor to that of white turnips. They are sometimes called Swedes and thought to be an accidental cross between a turnip and cabbage.

FRUIT

Every pantry should have a variety of fresh fruit on hand. Fruit is not only an important part of a balanced diet, it travels well, is generally eaten raw, and most fruit is the portion size that conforms to the fruit itself. There are several categories of fruit and seasons to match. In today's world of shopping in America, most fruit that is found in super markets is not already ripe and therefore requires advance purchase and ripening at home. The following is a short list of common fruit found in the American diet.

Citrus

Citrus fruit has been in existence for millennia. Typically they grow in tropical or sub-tropical climates, although some types of citrus grow well in China, Europe, and North America. The original four ancient species of citrus are mandarin, pomelo, citron, and papeda. All other species of citrus are genetic descendants of these four. Papeda does not resemble the other three in appearance. Some of the more common species that are derived from papeda are kaffir lime and yuzu. These species figure prominently in the cuisine of Southeast Asia and Micronesia. All citrus fruits are an important source of Vitamin C in the diet. Because of where they are grown, most citrus fruit is available year round.

Oranges are the most recognizable and most consumed of all citrus in America. Today's orange in all its varieties are genetically thought to be 75 percent pomelo and 25 percent mandarin. Most of the oranges in the American diet come from Florida; although California and Texas are also orange producing states. A very high percentage of oranges are converted into juice. After coffee, orange juice is the most popular breakfast beverage in America. The best juice orange is the Valencia, although blood oranges and cara cara (also known as pink or red navel) are excellent juicing oranges. Navel oranges are a fruit within a fruit, since the "navel" is actual a smaller version of the mother fruit and all the seeds are contained within this section. This quality makes a navel orange ideal for sectioning and eating.

Tangerines and **Clemetines** are direct descendants of mandarins. They are a bit smaller than oranges and not perfectly round. The sections separate with a portion of the inner skin, making them less messy than an orange to eat. Their seasonality makes them both a great winter source of citrus fruit and therefore Vitamin C. Halos are a type of mandarin grown mostly in California. They are treasured for their sweet taste and lack of seeds.

Grapefruits are considered to be the healthiest of all citrus by many dieticians. They were originally called Shattuck or Shattuck fruit, a reference to Captain

Shaddock who is credited with their accidental origin. They are a hybrid of the pomelo and the sweet orange. Through the years of their very short existence they have often been misidentified as a pomelo. They originate from Barbados, where Captain Shaddock accidentally crossed a pomelo with a sweet orange. The four major varieties are white, pink, Ruby Red, and Star Ruby. The difference between the four varieties is color and sweetness. Typically, the darker the color the sweeter the fruit is. Tangelos and Minneolas are hybrids of grapefruit.

Lemons and **limes** are often grouped together in cooking; however, they are distinctly different fruits with origins in different parts of the world. Both are direct descendants of citron. Lemons come from a small evergreen tree native to Asia. They are the second most consumed citrus fruit in America. Because of their aromatic smell, they have found their way into several non-culinary products, like furniture wax and dish detergent. They are used to make beverages and sauces and can serve as a great non-sodium condiment for fish and vegetables. Limes originate in Iraq. They are typically smaller than a lemon and green in color. Because they are picked immature, the limes that are found in the supermarket have little to no seeds. Varieties include Key lime and kaffir lime.

Stone Fruits

Stone fruits are probably the most diverse fruit group. Botanists refer to them as drupes. Members of the drupe family include **coconuts, coffee, olives, dates, mangoes, almonds, cherries, plums, peaches, apricots, and nectarines**. Walnuts and hickory nuts are also drupes. There are three categories of stone fruit-freestone, clingstone and tryma. Freestone drupes are fruits whose stones, or pits, can be removed with little or no harm to the flesh. These include certain varieties of cherries, peaches, plums, and nectarines. Freestone fruits are most suitable for direct consumption. Clingstone drupes are fruits whose flesh tends to cling to the pit when removing. These include the different varieties of those identified as freestone and also olives and dates. They are best suited for making jams.

Since they are so diverse, stone fruits have different growing seasons and can therefore be consumed year round. They are an important source of fiber. The most common types in the America diet are peaches, plums, cherries, apricots, and nectarines. **Peaches** and **nectarines** both originate in China and are virtually the same fruit. Peaches have a characteristic fuzzy finish to their skin while the skin of a nectarine is smooth. Along with cherries, apricots, almonds and plums, they are members of the rose family. They are excellent choices for fruit to go, as each fruit is a single serving.

Cherries are largely grown in the American Northwest and Michigan. They have a very short growing season so the consumer has to take advantage of them when they are in season, which is usually June. They are very closely related to almonds. There are three types: sweet, wild, and sour. Sweet cherries come in several varieties, with Bing being the most popular. Wild cherries can be any type of cherry that is not specifically cultivated. Sour cherries are used mainly for pies and other baked goods. They are higher acid and have a better nutritional profile than sweet cherries. Due to the short growing season cherries are often dried to preserve them. After World War II, the Japanese planted numerous cherry trees in Washington, DC. Their annual blossoming has since become one of the classic signs of spring's arrival in the nation's capital.

Apricots are the fruit of a small tree or bush native to Armenia. They are an important part of the Turkish and Iranian diet. They are heartier than either the peach or nectarine in that they can withstand cooler climates. Cultivars are generally grafted onto peach or plum trees for greater support; although the fruit itself remains the same. They are very amenable to being dried and preserved, making the dried version a perfect snack or a great addition to a school lunch. Dried apricots are often found in granola and other cereals. Reconstituted, they make excellent glazes for tarts.

Bananas

Americans love **bananas**. In fact, the expression "going bananas" implies over excitement. They are the largest herbaceous flowering plant in the world. While there are several types, most divide bananas into two groups, bananas and plantains. They grow in tropical regions, such as Africa, Central and South America, and Australia. They are one of the most common fruit snacks in the American diet. Because of transit time, bananas are picked when not ripe and shipped. They tend to ripen quickly after purchase, so the consumer should only purchase what can be consumed in 3–4 days time. Most fans of bananas have a rotation system for purchasing, ripening, and consuming. A truly ripe banana is very yellow with brown spots.

Bananas are an excellent addition to a bowl of morning cereal. Their sweet flavor and ease of packing make them a favorite for children's school lunches. Their soft texture makes them quite suitable for drinks, like shakes, smoothies, and daiquiries. They also find themselves in pies, ice cream, pudding, and other desserts. Bananas can be frozen when getting too ripe and can then be used for banana bread after thawing.

Bananas are monogenomic and are therefore susceptible to many diseases and parasites. The current genotype sold in the US was not widely cultivated until the variety that was popular before 1970 fell victim to disease and was all but rendered extinct. This process is almost certain to repeat itself in the future. Organizations like the Slow Food Movement have taken steps to preserve the heirloom seed stock.

Plantains are a larger, somewhat flatter variety of banana that are very starchy. They comprise an important part of the diet in many African countries. The two main varieties are yellow and green. The green type of plantain is used for savory dishes, while the yellow (which turns black) is used for sweet dishes. The most common method of preparation is frying. In both the sweet and savory versions, the plantain is peeled and cut into slices, then fried. Once fried, the slices are pounded thin and refried. Savory fried plantains are usually salted, while sweet fried plantains may be sprinkled with sugar and/or cinnamon.

Apples and Pears

With over 7,500 known cultivars, apples are among the most widely planted fruit species in the world. Over 80 million tons of apples were produced in 2013, with China, their historical point of origin, producing more than half. Apples have been a part of several tales of lore from a variety of cultures. The mythical Johnny Appleseed was an American nurseryman and conservationist of the eighteenth and nineteenth century whose real name was John Chapman. Through his nomadic lifestyle, he is credited with creating the root stock for many of the apple orchards in Pennsylvania, Ohio, Indiana, and Ontario. No historical reference to apples could be better known than that of the Biblical story of Adam and Eve and the temptation of the apple that led to their expulsion from paradise.

Apples have a variety of applications in cooking depending on their size, texture, and sweetness. Red and Golden Delicious apples are most often eaten raw and are a favorite for packed lunches. Macintosh apples are also great for munching. Granny Smith apples tend to be tart and firm and are therefore used mainly for cooking. Newer varieties of apples include Gala, Pink Lady, and Fuji. Apples tend to have a long shelf life and therefore can be purchased in bulk and stored at room temperature or in the refrigerator.

Apples are harvested practically year round. The harvest period is typically forty-five days or so, but it can be shorter or longer, depending on weather and variety. The summer crop includes Gala, Golden Supreme, McIntosh (although they are also harvested in fall), and Duchess. Fall varieties are Fuji, Golden Delicious, Red Delicious, and Gravenstein. The winter crop includes Granny Smith, King, and Greening.

There are two types of juices made from apples, apple cider and apple juice. A very large percentage of apple production is dedicated to making juice. Apple cider is a seasonal drink that is traditionally served in the fall. Apples that are freshly picked and sometimes overripe are crushed and squeezed to make the cider. The cider is not filtered and may or may not be pasteurized. Unpasteurized apple cider is generally served only at the orchards. Pasteurized apple cider is sold in supermarkets because it has a longer shelf life and is a safer product. Hard cider is the result of exposing the pressed cider to air and allowing airborne bacteria to ferment the juice. Hard cider contains alcohol. Apple cider vinegar can be made from cider by introducing acetobacter.

Apple juice is one of the most popular fruit juices in the US. It is consumed by people of all ages. Apple juice differs from apple cider in that, except in rare cases, it is filtered and pasteurized. The filtration process includes the use of a centrifuge. It may be further treated with enzymes to remove pectin and starch, which tend to help suspend particulate matter. Once the juice is pasteurized it may be bottled in aseptic containers and stored at room temperature. This is what has made apple juice so popular. Other products made from apples include apple sauce, apple jelly, and apple butter.

Pears are another member of the rose family. They are cultivated as ornamental in addition to fruit bearing trees. They are similar in texture to apples but more aromatic. Their origin is thought to be in China, although the word pear or its equivalent shows up in Latin and the ancient Celtic language. Trees are produced by grafting, sometimes onto its relative, the **quince.** Quince root stocks are preferred because they produce shorter trees and easier harvesting. There are over three thousand cultivars in existence today.

Pears, like apples, can be consumed raw or cooked. They are usually purchased unripe and require some ripening before eating. A pear is ripe when the skin gives to light pressure. Pears can be stored at room temperature or in the refrigerator. If refrigerated, they can last a couple of weeks. Several varieties of pears are poached in sweet court bouillon and served as a plated dessert. Bosc and Anjou pears are best suited for poaching. Pears show up in literature and song. In Homer's *Odyssey*, they are found in the sublime orchard of Alcinus. And who can forget that "partridge in a pear tree" in the Christmas carol "Twelve Days of Christmas"? Pears are also canned after poaching and squeezed to make pear juice. Poire is an exquisite after dinner digestif with a whole pear contained in the bottle. The bottles are placed around the blossoms before the pear appears to achieve this effect.

GRAINS

Rice

Rice is a grass grain of the genus *Oryza*. There are twenty valid species of rice. *Oryza sativa* is the major species of rice found in Asia. Three sub-species of *sativa* correspond to areas where they are currently grown. They are: *Indica*, grown on the Indian subcontinent (we refer to this variety as Basmati rice); *Sinica*, grown largely in Japan (a short grain rice that is used to make sushi); and *Japanica*, grown mostly in Indonesia.

Types of rice that may be more familiar to consumers are as follows:

- Long grain rice—the most popular variety in the US is grown throughout the world, especially in the Southern part of the US.
- Short grain rice—grown in the Po Valley in Italy and used to make risotto. Sushi rice is also short grain.
- Brown rice—rice with the bran still intact.

- Wild Rice—not rice, but a cousin of the genus *Oryza*. It grows along the muddy bottoms of brackish water and is the exclusive right of harvest of the American Indian.

Milling

The purpose of milling is to remove the hulls and bran from the harvested rice. After removal of the hulls, the rice is called brown rice, a reference not to color but to the fact that the bran has not been removed. Brown rice is then milled in a milling machine to remove the bran and produce white rice. Sometimes rice is steamed before milling for the purpose of retaining more nutrients. This is called converted rice.

Nutritional Data

Nutritional data on rice has been compiled since 1909, when it was suggested that consumption of rice whose outer layers had been removed by milling (white rice) was the cause of beriberi, a disease caused by thiamin deficiency. Analysis of brown rice and white rice shows brown rice to be higher in all nutrients except carbohydrates. Concentrations of thiamin and fat are five times greater in brown rice than in white rice. In addition, fiber, niacin, phosphorous, potassium, sodium, iron, and riboflavin levels are two to three times greater in brown rice than in white rice. This loss of nutrients is directly attributable to the milling and polishing process, which literally scrapes the nutrients away. For this reason, it is far better nutritionally to consume brown rice than white rice.

Quinoa

Quinoa is known as the super grain of the Incas. It was first domesticated in the Andean region of Peru and around Lake Titicaca three thousand to four thousand years ago. It is a close relative of **amarynth**, also considered to be a super grain. Other relatives include buck wheat, spinach, and beet roots. Like amarynth, the leaves are edible; however, availability in the US is limited. The seeds are washed after harvest to remove the bitter coating.

Quinoa is nutritionally significant because of its high essential amino acid content, especially lysine. It is therefore an important source of complete proteins for vegans.

Quinoa is prepared much the same way as rice and other grains. Simply boiling it in water or stock softens the grain to the point of palatability. Like rice, herbs, flavorings, and vegetables are often added to cooked quinoa to produce a complete dish. Cooked quinoa can also be chilled and served in a salad, such as the popular kale and quinoa salad.

CHAPTER FOUR

Meat, Fish, and Poultry

MEAT

Beef

Beef is the All-American meat. Due to the relative abundance of high quality beef in the US, the American appetite for this red meat is unequalled. The entire sequence of raising, slaughtering, processing, and shipping has become so efficient that most Americans can purchase choice beef at reasonable and relatively stable prices.

The United States Department of Agriculture (USDA) inspects all beef to ensure that the animals are free of diseases, parasites, and open sores at the time of slaughter. Some beef is then graded by trained personnel who are paid by the processor. Grading is optional. The grader makes a cut between the twelfth and thirteenth rib and grades the entire animal on these observations. The criteria for grading are **marbling, firmness, color,** and **texture**. The eight grades for steers, heifers, and cows, listed in descending order of quality are: **Prime, Choice, Good (sometimes called Select), Standard, Commercial, Utility, Cutter,** and **Canner.** Only four to five percent of graded beef is Prime and most of this meat is sold to the restaurant industry. Only the top three grades are sold as is to the public. The other grades are used in processed foods, animal feed and other products.

The beef carcass is broken down into **eight or nine primal cuts**, depending on the source. They are: **shank, chuck, brisket, rib, plate, short loin, flank, sirloin,** and **round.** Some sources list the short loin and sirloin together and others list the shank as part of the chuck. In the early days of meatpacking, most beef was shipped to regional meat markets as sides, or quarters. From there, the butchers would break down the sides or quarters into sub-primal cuts. Modern shipping has required most packing plants to ship only boxed beef to point-of-sale markets. Meat cutters then break down the boxed beef into retail cuts.

Each of the primal cuts of beef is broken down into sub-primal cuts and finally into retail cuts. Many retail cuts are complete sub-primal cuts. Just to add to the confusion, there are what are referred to as marketing forms of meat. These cuts are mostly what consumers see in the meat department of the grocery store. The terms used to describe them vary widely across the US. In some cases, boxed beef is fabricated into different marketing cuts in different areas, thereby eliminating the availability of certain cuts in certain regions. In other cases, an identical cut of meat will have a different name for the purposes of marketing. A Delmonico Steak in Pennsylvania may be called a Kansas City Steak in St. Louis or a ribeye in Texas. A Romanian Steak in New Jersey may be called a Skirt Steak in New Mexico. Tri-tip roasts, which are very popular on the West coast may be hard to come by on the retail level on the East coast because this cut (beef knuckle or sirloin tip) is usually fabricated into steaks.

What follows is a description of the sub-primal cuts of beef, along with some marketing cuts, and a brief description of what the cuts are used for in cooking. Beginning with the upper anterior, the **chuck** contains the first five of the thirteen ribs. Most butchers label these ribs 1–5, although some label them exactly opposite (9–13). Most cuts of chuck are well marbled, therefore quite tasty. Since this is a working region of the animal, most cuts are not very tender. The exception is the **boneless chuck eye roast**, which is the anterior extension of the ribeye. This cut is sometimes broken down into steaks, with a marketing name of **mock tenderloin** or **flat iron steak**. **Blade roast** or steak is found in the same area and may be used for braising or marinated and broiled. The top anterior portion of the chuck is usually used for stew beef. **Cross rib roast** is used for pot roast. The five **short ribs** contained within the chuck may be marinated and grilled or braised. **Boneless shoulder** and **arm roast** or steak are usually used for pot roast or otherwise braised. Steaks may be marinated, grilled, and sliced. The remainder of the chuck, including trim, is converted to ground beef.

The **shank**, or **foreshank** is the front leg portion of the steer. The muscles are therefore worked quite hard and subsequently the meat is not tender. The bones are rich with albumen and make excellent stocks and soups. **Shank cross cut** is very well suited for hearty soup or stew. Shank meat may be braised like short ribs or put into a stew. What little trim is associated with the shank may be used for ground beef.

Directly below the chuck and posterior to the shank is the **brisket.** Along with chuck and rib, brisket has the highest fat percentage on a beef carcass. It is therefore very tasty, although most retailers in this day and age trim large amounts of the fat in deference to dietary concerns. Brisket is not a tender cut and is therefore best suited for braising and other wet techniques of cooking. Slow dry cooking, such as barbecued brisket or slow-baked brisket, also yields a tender product. A large percentage of brisket meat is **corned**; a process of brining and preserving that helps to tenderize. **Corned beef brisket**, either whole, trimmed, or flat portion is slowly poached and often served sliced in deli sandwiches or served with cabbage and potatoes as a traditional St. Patrick's Day meal.

Directly posterior to the chuck is the **rib.** The rib includes seven ribs, numbers 6–12. Most cuts within the rib are considered to be of very high quality and are therefore suitable for dry cooking, like roasting or broiling. The rib roast is fabricated and marketed in many forms under many names. A **bone-in rib roast** is sometimes called a **standing rib roast** and may contain all seven ribs or as few as two. The **large end rib roast** is closest to the chuck and very flavorful, but the ratio of deckle to ribeye is very high. A **deckle** is a piece of meat that surrounds an interior cut of meat. In the case of the rib, this very fatty, yet tasty deckle is sometimes referred to as the **lip.** A **small end rib roast** is considered to be of higher quality than the large end, since the deckle to ribeye ratio is smaller. Many consider only the small end as worthy of being called **prime rib.** Most restaurants purchase whole ribs, either bone-in or **oven-ready boneless** and market them as prime rib. Almost all restaurants purchase the rib roast with the lip on. When the lip is removed, the roast is usually called a **ribeye roast.** Most boneless rib roasts are categorized according to weight. Most restaurants purchase **twelve and up** or **thirteen and up** oven-ready boneless rib roasts. These terms imply that each roast weighs at least twelve or at least thirteen pounds.

This factor is important to restaurants because of plate coverage. Rib roasts may be cut into steaks and marketed bone-in or boneless. A boneless rib steak is referred to as **a ribeye steak** or a **Delmonico steak,** although some believe a true Delmonico steak is only the thirteenth rib, which is in the short loin. In some regions of the country, it is called a **Kansas City Steak**. Seven **short ribs** are located in the rib and they are suitable for braising or marinating and broiling.

The **plate** is located directly below the rib and is the diaphragm muscle. Some butchers include the seven short ribs from the rib in this cut. The cut would then be called the **short plate**. The plate is divided into an inner muscle and an outer muscle. The inner muscle is referred to as **hanger steak.** It is more tender than the outer muscle, which is called **skirt steak.** In the Eastern US, skirt steak is marinated and grilled and called **Romanian Steak**. In the West and Southwest, it is similarly marinated and grilled, then sliced for **fajitas.** This cut has historically been very economic. In the 1980s, marketers across the country discovered the broad appeal of fajitas and capitalized on this trend, resulting in a tripling of the retail price for skirt steak. Although in the past the plate was sometimes used for stew beef and ground beef, the economic impact of the fajita craze has virtually eliminated this practice.

Directly posterior to the plate is the **flank,** one of the three boneless primal cuts of beef. Flank steak went through a marketing makeover similar to that of skirt steak, although further in the past. Until the early 1960s, flank steak was economic and was sold whole, in rolls, or as ground beef. Marketers then discovered that **London Broil** had a potentially broad-based appeal in the US. They began to market flank steak as the only cut to make true London Broil and the price soared. Because of the low yield (3–4 lbs. per carcass), flank steak is now sold mostly to restaurants in cryovaced multiples of three.

Directly posterior to the rib is the **short loin**. The short loin contains some of the most prized cuts of beef. The thirteenth rib is located in the short loin. The cut is divided into two portions, the **shell** and the **tenderloin**. When steaks are cut with both portions intact, including the bone, they are called, from anterior to posterior, **club steak (also called top loin steak), T-bone steak,** and **Porterhouse steak**. The chief difference between the three is the portion of tenderloin in each. Club steak contains almost no tenderloin, Porterhouse contains the largest portion, and T-bone is somewhere between the two. Many consider the first cut, which contains the thirteenth rib, to be a true **Delmonico steak**.

When the filet is removed and the bone is not, all three steaks would be called **shell steaks**. When the bone is removed, they would be referred to as **boneless top loin, strip steak, New York sirloin, New York strip,** and sometimes **Kansas City Steak** or **Kansas City Strip**. The latter two names have caused perhaps the most confusion in beef nomenclature. Depending on where you are, a Kansas City steak could be a shell steak, a strip steak, a club steak, a Delmonico, or a ribeye. In Kansas City, it is almost always a large rib steak.

The **tenderloin,** or **filet,** is the only sub-primal cut of beef to span two primal cuts, the short loin and the sirloin. The largest portion is in the sirloin. The filet is trimmed by removing the long, thin **chain** and trimming the excess fat and silverskin. About one-fourth to one-third of the small end is removed and used for tenderloin tips. The rest is either cut into steaks, referred to as **tenderloins, filets,** or **filet mignon,** or roasted whole and called **chateaubriand.**

The **sirloin** is located directly posterior to the short loin. The meat is well marbled and suitable for dry cooking like roasting or broiling. It contains the largest portion of filet. When the filet is left intact, which only occurs in hanging beef (very rare these days), it is cut into **pin-bone, flat-bone,** and **wedge-bone steaks,** from anterior to posterior. When the filet is removed, it is referred to as **boneless sirloin** or **sirloin butt,** which is divided into **top sirloin** and **bottom sirloin.** Top and bottom sirloin is often used for London Broil. **Top butt steak** is used in restaurants, often marinated and grilled, and comes with many marketing names, or simply as a boneless sirloin. The portion of the filet that is located in the sirloin is referred to as **tenderloin butt.** Since the filet that is in the short loin is often sold with the T-bone, Porterhouse and club steaks, the tenderloin butt is frequently sold separately, often cryovaced with two per package. The **tip** or **half-tip,** is usually cut into steaks. In some parts of the country, it is left whole and sold along with the tip located in the round, as **tri-tip roast.** Sirloin trim is sometimes used for ground beef.

The **round** is located at the very rear of the animal. The cuts span the quality range from those that are suitable for broiling, frying, and roasting to braising cuts, stew beef, and ground beef. A **steamship round,** mostly served in restaurants and catering functions as a marketing and presentation tool, is the entire round, minus the shank. **Top round** is usually roasted or cut into steaks that may be breaded and fried as chicken-fried steak. **Bottom round** is usually braised or roasted and sometimes cut into steaks that may be similarly breaded and fried.

Eye round is excellent for roasting and is sometimes cut into steaks, marinated and broiled. **Cubed steak** is made from all three cuts: top, bottom, and eye round. The **heel** is very flavorful and may be roasted or braised. The **rump** is most frequently roasted and may also be braised. The **shank** is used for soups, stews, and braising. The **tip,** or **knuckle,** is used for **tip steaks,** kabobs, and roasts, either for roasting or braising. If combined with the half-tip found in the sirloin, it is called **tri-tip roast.** All portions of the round, including trim, may be used for ground beef.

Chicken

Chicken is considered by the meat packing industry to be poultry. According to the United States Department of Agriculture (USDA), poultry is grouped according to kind and class. Kind refers to the species, such as chicken, turkey, duck or goose. Class refers to features such as age, sex, and physical characteristics. The classes of chickens are as follows:

- **Fryer or Broiler**—a young chicken of either sex, usually 9–16 weeks old. It has tender meat, pliable skin, and flexible breastbone cartilage. A **Rock Cornish Game Hen** is a young chicken, usually 5–7 weeks of age, less than two pounds dressed weight and the offspring of a Cornish chicken or Cornish chicken mix.
- **Roaster**—a young chicken of either sex, usually 3–5 months old. The skin and flesh are similar in texture to a fryer, but the breastbone cartilage is less flexible.
- **Stag**—a male chicken less than 10 months old, with coarse skin, toughened flesh, and somewhat hard breastbone cartilage. Maturity is somewhat less than that of a cock or rooster.
- **Hen, Stewing Chicken** or **Fowl**—a mature female, usually over 10 months old, with meat that is less tender than a roaster and a non-flexible breast bone.
- **Cock** or **Rooster**—a mature male, usually over 10 months old, with coarse skin, tough and dark meat, and hardened breast tip.

Although most classes of chicken may conceivably be cooked by frying, roasting, broiling, or stewing, it is most advisable to use the name of the class to determine the cooking technique that is best suited. Fryers and broilers should be cut into small pieces and fried, broiled, sautéed or baked. A whole fryer or broiler may also be roasted, but the yield is usually small and the process of stuffing, roasting, and carving is better suited to a larger bird, such as a roaster. Older birds, like stags, cocks, and stewing hens are best prepared by stewing since the meat is not as tender as that of a younger bird.

To break a chicken down into its parts, start by removing the back. Use a heavy chef knife and make an initial cut alongside the neck end, pressing firmly and drawing the knife through until you reach the tail end. Repeat the process with the other side of the back to remove it. The chicken should be quite flexible at this point and you should be able to spread it out flat on a cutting board. Remove both legs and cut into drumstick and thigh, if desired. Remove both wings and cut into drumette, wing and tip, if desired. Invert the breast by applying pressure with both thumbs on the inside, exposing the reddish-colored sternum. Remove this bone and cut the breast in half or quarters.

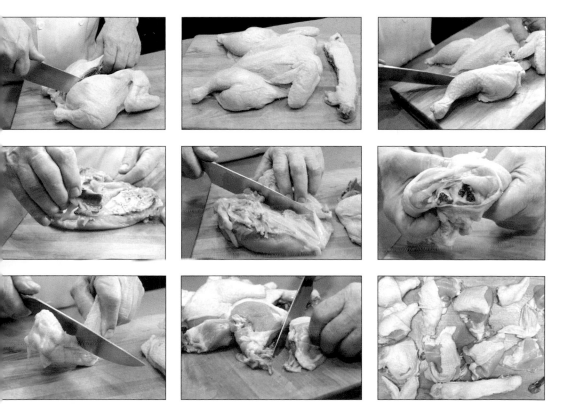

Pork

Pork is the second most popular meat source in the US, behind beef. Unlike beef or lamb, hogs are bred exclusively for their meat. Therefore, pork tends to be very tender, since hogs are consistently younger at the time of slaughter. This factor has also contributed greatly to the decline of the foremost detraction to pork consumption—trichinosis. Trichinosis is an affliction caused by eating the flesh of omnivores, such as pork and bear that has been infected with the trichina worm. The worm generally enters the host via the digestive tract and, if unchecked, eventually spreads to the muscle tissue. Eating the meat or muscle tissue of such an animal would therefore transfer the worm to a new host. Since hogs are generally slaughtered at six months, any infected animals would most likely not have worms in their muscle tissue or meat. Since there are still a handful of cases of human trichinosis reported in the US each year, pork should be cooked to an internal temperature of 145°F. Other methods of ensuring safe pork are curing and smoking, as with bacon and ham, freezing at 0°F for thirty days or more, and lowering the temperature to -35°F for any length of time.

The pork carcass is divided into four primal cuts, although many butchers consider there to be six. The standard primal cuts from anterior to posterior are: **pork shoulder, Boston butt, pork loin, pork ham.** Primal cuts are broken down into retail cuts. The **jowl**, located in the head region is generally used to make sausage or add fat to prepared foods. **Pig's feet** are considered to be only the front feet. They are sometimes pickled or otherwise cured and smoked and used as flavorings. The **picnic shoulder** is the bottom half of what would be the chuck on a beef carcass. This contains **fresh and smoked picnic arm, arm roast, ham hocks, neck bones, and arm steak.** Much of this section is ground and marketed as is or made into sausage. The **clear plate** is located in the same position as the plate on a beef carcass. **Fat back** and **lard** come from the clear plate. The **Boston Shoulder** is the upper portion of what would be the chuck on a beef carcass. **Blade Boston roast, smoked shoulder roll**, and **cubed steak** come from this cut.

The **loin** contains the most prized cuts on the pork carcass. It spans an area that would include the rib, short loin and sirloin on a beef carcass. A whole pork loin is one of the best buys any retailer can make. **Country style spare ribs, blade chops, baby back ribs, Canadian style bacon, loin chops, boneless and**

bone-in loin roast, tenderloin, rib chops, sirloin chops, and **boneless top loin roast** come from the loin. It is particularly frugal to purchase a whole boneless pork loin and break it down to portion sizes. Since there is no bone, it does not require the skills of a butcher to do so. A whole boneless pork loin will yield sixteen portions of meat if fabricated correctly.

Pork bellies are the equivalent of the short plate on a beef carcass. **Spare ribs, slab bacon, sliced bacon,** and **salt pork** come from this cut. **Hams** are usually smoked to overcome the characteristic strong flavor. The ham is divided into **shank and butt** portion. The butt generally has more meat to bone. **Ham hocks** are usually smoked and used for flavoring.

Many of the smoked and lower grade cuts of pork are used for seasoning and in the manufacture of sausage. Bacon, fat back, salt pork, hog jowls, ham hocks, pigs feet and neck bones are all used for this purpose. Bacon is, of course, one of the most popular breakfast meats in the US. Premium cuts, such as chops are fried, broiled or sautéed. Larger cuts, like ham or loin roast are most often slow roasted or baked. Many cuts, especially ribs, are barbecued, either in an oven or outdoor grill. Whole pigs are roasted and served with great fanfare in many cultures. Suckling pig (less than thirty pounds, unweaned) is a holiday favorite.

SEAFOOD

Seafood includes **fish, shellfish, crustaceans,** and **invertebrates**. Although the name implies that seafood comes only from the sea, or salt water, it also includes many freshwater species from rivers, streams, lakes, and ponds. Seafood is and has been consumed the world round since prehistoric days. In many parts of the world, especially Japan and Asia, it is often eaten raw. Since the varieties are so diverse and so perishable, cooks need to know how to purchase, store, fabricate, and cook seafood in order to successfully serve it.

The process of preparing seafood in modern times starts with a visit to the local fishmonger (a person who sells seafood). It is always a good idea to get to know this person by asking questions about where and when they purchase their seafood and what types of seafood they generally carry. Developing a rapport with your fishmonger by telling them what types of seafood you're interested in before the day you purchase it will help to ensure freshness.

Use your nose as the first indicator that the seafood in your local market is fresh. The protein in seafood decomposes rapidly, breaking down into the amino acids that comprise them and subsequently releasing a characteristic ammonia-like odor. If you smell a strong odor like this, you may want to switch fishmongers. Use your eyes as the next indicator of freshness. **Whole fish** should look firm and glossy, with clear eyes. Skin should have an even sheen with scales intact. Gills should be red and moist. **Fillets** should be firm, clean cut, and not bruised. Finally, use your hands to touch the fish. Whole fish should have a clear sheen on the surface. The fish should be firm to the touch with few exceptions.

The best way to store fresh fish is on ice. The temperature of ice (32°F) is the perfect temperature for preserving freshness. Be sure to provide a means of draining the water that results from the melting ice so that the fish is not stored in water. Fillets should be wrapped in plastic and stored on top of ice.

Shellfish are generally sold live or shucked. Shells should not be open, with the exception of certain species of oysters. Shells should close when tapped with the fingers. Some bivalves, like oysters and clams, are shucked and sold fresh. Be sure to ask your fishmonger when they were shucked and use your nose to judge freshness. Fresh shellfish should be scrubbed clean in running water with a stiff brush and then soaked in fresh water with cornmeal to passivate them. This process causes the shellfish to expel any sand or foreign material. Mussels contain a seaweed-like "beard' which must be removed just prior to cooking. This is located between the two shells and removing it causes the mussel to die. Therefore, the mussels should be cooked immediately after removing the beards. Shellfish whose shells do not open upon cooking should be discarded.

Crustaceans include lobsters, shrimp, crab, langoustines, and **crawfish.** With the exception of shrimp, they are generally sold and cooked live or directly after the kill. There are three species of coldwater **lobsters.** The American lobster or *Homarus americanus* is harvested in the North Atlantic waters of Maine and Canada. This is the lobster that most Americans boil or steam whole. Across the Atlantic, in Ireland, Scotland, England and parts of Scandinavia two species, *Homarus vulgaris* and *Homarus gamarus*, are found in relatively small numbers. The anatomy of all three is very similar and most distinctly noted for their large claws. The season for North Atlantic hard shell lobster is April 15 to June 30 and October 15 to December 31. **Rock lobsters,** also called spiny lobsters, are native to the warmer waters of Australia, South Africa, the Caribbean, and the

Mediterranean. They are not of the same genus as true lobsters. They have large tails and almost no claws. The genus and species is *Palinarus vulgaris*, a close relative of the crawfish. They are sometimes called langoustines or *langouste*. Lobsters are boiled or steamed whole and served with drawn butter. They are also stuffed and baked or broiled. The tails, especially of rock lobsters, are also steamed or broiled and served with drawn butter. The meat is used for bisque and other dishes like Lobster Newburg and Lobster Thermidor.

There are numerous species of **crabs**, both cold and warm water. They include blue crab, stone crab, Dungeness crab and king crab. Crabs are usually cooked soon after they are caught or sold live for cooking. The meat of the cooked crab is removed and packaged in plastic containers or pasteurized and canned. The crab that is packaged in plastic tubs is refrigerated and sold quickly. If not sold directly, the same crab is then frozen for future sale. Crab is boiled or steamed and served with drawn butter or chilled with cocktail sauce. The meat can also be used in a variety of dishes, most notably crab cakes, Crab Mornay, and bisque. Soft shell crab is crab that is caught between molting its shell and growing a new one. They are usually sautéed or breaded and fried.

Except in states where **shrimp** is harvested, like Texas, Louisiana, and Georgia, most shrimp is frozen before shipping. Fresh shrimp may be sold head on or head off. Only the freshest shrimp can be sold with the heads on, since they separate from the body within 24–48 hours after dying. Shrimp is sized according to the average number per pound. Typical sizes are over 50 (popcorn shrimp), 40–50 (small shrimp), 30–40 (medium shrimp), 26–30 (large shrimp), 21–25 (jumbo shrimp) and 16–20 (colossal shrimp). Larger than 16–20 shrimp are sold as "under" a certain number per pound, such as under 15, under 12, under 10, and under 7. These shrimp are sometimes referred to as **prawns**, although Europeans only use this term to describe a **crustacean** of a specific point of origin. Shrimp is one of the most versatile types of seafood from the standpoint of preparation. They are typically boiled or steamed and served cold with cocktail sauce, fried, and broiled. Larger shrimp are sometimes stuffed and baked or broiled. Shrimp are also used in a wide variety of dishes including gumbo, jambalaya, paella, and stir-fries.

The anatomy of true fish falls into two categories: flat fish and round fish. Examples of flat fish are sole, flounder, and fluke. Examples of round fish are salmon, trout, and snapper. Unless cooked whole, most fish are filleted before cooking.

The procedure is different for flat fish versus round fish. For flat fish, use a fillet knife to cut straight to the spine along the lateral line. Turn the knife sideways and follow the bones to remove each fillet. There will be two fillets on each side. For round fish, cut straight down to the spine directly posterior to the gills. Turn the knife sideways and follow the bones to remove each fillet. There will be one fillet per side. On larger fish, like salmon, you must then remove the pin bones by slowly withdrawing them with a pair of needle nose pliers or hemostats. Even larger fish, like swordfish, halibut, and grouper are cut into steaks. These are merely very large fillets that are additionally cut into portions by slicing directly into the fillet and removing the meat.

The size and type of fish determine the cooking technique for that fish. Smaller white flesh fish, like **flounder, sole, and Pompano** can be poached, sautéed or fried. Oilier hearty flavored fish like **salmon, mackerel and bluefish** are better grilled, especially after marinating. This cooking technique will help to overcome the hearty, often "fishy' flavor of these fish. For larger steak fish, like **swordfish and halibut**, broiling and grilling work best. Some intermediate size fish, especially salmon, can be poached whole, chilled, and served in a buffet with a cold sauce. Many small fish, like **trout and small flounder** can be pan-fried, smoked, or sautéed whole.

CHAPTER FIVE

Other Sources of Protein

DAIRY

Dairy products are an important source of protein and a wide variety of other nutrients, especially for those who do not get their protein from meat. Milk can come from several animal sources, such as goats and sheep, but the vast majority of dairy consumed in the US is cow's milk and products made from same. In this day and age, dairy products have the added advantage of choosing the fat level of the product you purchase. Aside from milk itself, dairy products include cheeses, yogurt, cream, butter, and ice cream.

Milk

Milk is consumed by over 6 billion people throughout the world. Initially, only infants could consume milk because adults lost the ability to produce lactase, the enzyme that metabolizes milk sugar, or lactose. A chance mutation, assumed to be centered in Europe, changed all that several thousand years ago. Most adults, therefore, can consume milk and dairy products without consequence. There are still many adults and children who are lactose intolerant and take lactase pills when consuming dairy or avoid them altogether.

Milk is an emulsion of fat and water based materials. In its natural form, it tends to separate into two layers, fat on top, aqueous on the bottom. This process is exacerbated under lower temperatures. In the days of home delivered milk, one would often find the loose fitting tops of the bottles pushed off by the fat layer on cold days. In today's world, milk is homogenized so that the two layers are virtually inseparable. Milk can be purchased as whole milk, 2 percent and 1 percent fat content or skim milk, which has no appreciable fat content. Aside from being a great source of protein and calcium, milk contains high levels of several vitamins and is fortified with Vitamin D.

Cream

Cream is the high fat layer of milk that is skimmed off before milk is homogenized. Commercially, milk is placed in a centrifuge to accelerate this process. Cream that is derived from this process is referred to as **sweet cream**. Cream is also derived from whey, which is a by-product of cheese manufacturing. This type of cream is lower in fat. In the US, cream is sold as the following products.

- **Half and Half**—10.5–18% butterfat; used for tea and coffee
- **Light Cream**—19–30% butterfat; used for sauces and soups, but also for whipping
- **Whipping Cream**—30–36% butterfat; used for whipping
- **Heavy Cream**—> 36% butterfat; used for producing stiff peak whipped cream

Yogurt

Yogurt is milk that has been cultured and thickened due to the introduction and incubation of lactic acid forming bacteria. These bacteria fall into three groups. *Lactobacillus Bulgaricus* and *Lactobacillus Acidophilus* are both protein coagulants and *Streptococcus Thermophilus* converts lactose (milk sugar) to lactic acid, which in turn coagulates milk proteins. These bacteria are typically introduced to milk by using a small amount of yogurt with active cultures (unpasteurized). Dry milk powder is added to create body except when making *kefir*, a type of acidophilus yogurt that is the consistency of a milkshake.

Several conditions must be met to produce quality yogurt. Equipment must be sterilized to prevent contamination from competing bacteria. Containers should be kept covered for the same reason. Milk (pasteurized) should be as fresh as possible and incubation must take place in an undisturbed environment with precise temperature control for an extended period (six to twelve hours).

This last requirement is best achieved in a home kitchen by using an electronic yogurt maker.

Cheese

Cheese is made from milk that has been acidified to produce its two constituent parts—**curds and whey.** The curd contains **casein,** or milk protein and fat. In most applications the milk is further treated with the enzyme rennet for greater yield. Certain simple cheeses, like cottage or farmer's cheese and the Indian cheese *paneer*, are simply made by acidifying the milk and straining. Indications are that cheese has been made for ten thousand years.

There are hundreds of varieties of cheese. The basic categories of cheese are **soft**—like Gouda, boursin, and brie; **hard**—like Parmagiano, aged cheddar, and Romano; and **bleu**—like Stilton Roquefort and gorgonzola. Other ways of categorizing cheese include fat content and fresh or aged.

Hard cheeses are often grated and used as toppings for pasta, vegetables, bread, and rice. **Parmagiano-Reggiano** is perhaps the most prized grating cheese in the world and it is named after the town and region of origin. Soft cheeses are usually consumed as is. **Mozzarella**, or stretched cheese, is made simply by heating the curd to 160°F and stretching. String cheese is a form of mozzarella that lends itself to easy packing and snacking, putting it high on the list of items to have on hand in the modern kitchen. **Bleu cheeses** have blue to green streaks of mold. They have a distinct salty and sometimes pungent flavor that is treasured by cheese lovers.

Butter

Butter is made by churning milk or cream to separate the butterfat from the protein. Butter made from pasteurized cream or milk is referred to as **sweet cream butter.** This is the preferred butter consumed in the US. Butter made from raw milk is called **raw cream butter.** This is sometimes called European style butter, as it is the preferred type of butter in Europe. The latter type has a very short shelf life of two weeks or so. Sweet cream butter can be kept frozen for up to one year or stored in a refrigerator for three months.

Before the days of refrigeration, butter was often salted to extend the shelf life. Because of this history, many are still of the opinion that salted butter is made from lower quality sweet, or unsalted butter. There is no specific credible indication that this is true in today's world. Butter is currently salted because people got used to the flavor of salted butter when used as a spread and they developed a taste for it. When stocking a refrigerator, the general rule is that **salted butter is used for the table**, largely as a spread, and **unsalted butter is used for cooking.**

LEGUMES

Legumes include **peanuts, dried beans, and soy**. They are an important source of protein for the meat-free diet. They are devoid of many of the unhealthy properties of animal protein, like saturated fat and cholesterol. Dried legumes in particular have long shelf lives, require no refrigeration, and are inexpensive.

Soy

The term soy is used to define any product that is derived from soy beans. This includes **tofu, soy milk, tempeh, soy sauce, and fermented bean paste.** Soy beans are also pressed to make soybean oil. Soy is considered by many to be a complete source of protein, as it contains high levels of the essential amino acids that are typically found in meat.

Soy milk is made by soaking dried soybeans in water, grinding them to extract the protein, and filtering to attain a white liquid similar in color and viscosity to cow's milk. It has been a staple of the Asian diet for centuries. It is low in fat and high in protein and, unlike cow's milk, does not contain lactose. It is used as a substitute for infant formula or cow's milk for babies who are lactose intolerant. It has become popular in recent years in the US because it contains a similar level of protein as cow's milk, much less fat, no cholesterol, and it is not from an animal source.

Tofu (called *dofu* or *daifu* in Chinese) is coagulated soy milk. It is also called **bean curd**. It is used extensively in Asian cuisine because of its versatility and vegetable source. There are several types of tofu. The difference between them is the moisture content. **Silken or soft tofu** is unfiltered and has the highest moisture level of all tofu. It has a texture to match its name. Within the category, there are several textures and moisture levels, including soft and firm. It is used to make both sweet and savory dishes. It is usually not cooked and is often eaten with a spoon as opposed to chop sticks due to its consistency.

Firm silken tofu should not be confused with **firm tofu**, which is silken tofu that has been strained and pressed. Firm tofu is packed in the water it was extracted from, just as silken tofu is. It is used in soups and some stir-fries. **Extra firm tofu** has the lowest moisture content of all fresh tofu. Due to its consistency, it is most often used for stir frying. **Fried tofu** is firm tofu that has been cut and deep fried. It is much lighter than fresh tofu and is a standard ingredient of the classic Thai dish Pad Thai.

Tempeh is made from whole fermented soybeans that are pressed and bound into a cake. The fermentation process gives it a more pronounced flavor than tofu. The binding process produces a cake that is similar in texture to meat. It is very popular in Indonesia, where it was invented, and also in Java. Because of its texture and richer taste it is used as a meat substitute in Asia and is becoming very popular in vegetarian cuisine in the US. It is actually higher in protein than tofu.

Dried Beans, Lentils, and Peas

Dried beans and lentils come from the same source. They are all seeds that are extracted from plant pods and dried. They have a long shelf life, can be stored at room temperature and are relatively inexpensive. They are most often used in soups, although Indians have a wide range of uses for lentils, which they call *daal*. Since they are dried, they sometimes require long simmering times when preparing them. This time can be shortened by soaking them in water in advance or they can be prepared in a pressure cooker.

Dried Beans
Dried beans come in many varieties. They are either **round or oval** shaped. **Red beans** are one half of the Cajun dish Red Beans and Rice. They are also cooked and crushed to make refried beans. **Pinto beans** are a staple of Texas cuisine and are served alongside competition chili (contains no beans) and at barbecues. **Kidney beans** are served in salads, like three-bean salad, and also in home style chili. **Black beans** are the star of Cuban black bean soup. They are also one of the components of "mud," the ubiquitous plate liner of Southwestern cuisine. There are many types of **white beans. Garbanzos** or **chick peas** are used in salads

and paella and are the chief ingredient in falafel. **Navy beans** and **Great North-ern beans** are usually used to make soup. **Canellini** or **white kidney beans** are used in Spanish salads and minestrone. Dried beans require the longest cooking time of all the dried legumes so they should be soaked in water before use.

Dried Peas

Dried peas are round when whole. They are used in soups and salads. **Black-eyed peas** are frequently served in soul food restaurants and throughout the south. They are traditionally eaten on New Year's for good luck. **Split peas** are whole dried peas that have been split in half. Dried peas do not usually take as long to cook as dried beans, but prior soaking can reduce the cooking time.

Lentils

There are approximately twenty varieties of lentils, or daal, in the Indian diet. **Moong daal** is a yellow lentil that is cooked and served as a side dish. **Chan-nah daal** is typically bright orange and usually cooked, pureed and served with grill onions and cumin seed. **French lentils** are the most common lentil in the Western diet. They are greenish gray and are usually used to make lentil soup. **Umbrian lentils** are prized for their rich flavor. They are brown and used to make stew and soup.

Where and When to Shop

Now that you have some background information on cook's ingredients, *it's time to shop!* Your first decision will be **where to shop.** If you are interested in pur-chasing organic food or food that comes from responsible sources, mostly local, Whole Foods Market is a national chain that has a decades long reputation for being an informed source for all of the above. Trader Joe's is also a national chain that has similarly sourced food; however, sometimes not as many choices as WFM. Other local stores that have quality food supplies at reasonable prices are Wegman's and Publix. If you have the freezer space or you need higher vol-umes of staples, you may want to shop at one of the bulk food stores like BJ's, Sam's Club, or Costco. You will probably get the lowest prices at these stores, but if you end up throwing away some of the food because it's more than you can use, these savings evaporate quickly. In tandem with purchasing large portions of freezer friendly food, like meat, you may wish to purchase a vacuum sealer to extend their shelf life. In all cases, food should be used by using the acronym—

FIFO—First in; first out

What this means is that all food should be rotated, so that the oldest is used first. When stocking the pantry, don't over shop. Try to develop an organized shopping list by having a list of staples that you should always have on hand and what their desired stocking level is. In a professional kitchen, this is referred to as par stocks. In order to properly shop, you should take an inventory of these items to determine if you need to replenish them and if so, how much it will take to reach the desired stocking level. Supplement your shopping list with items that are specific to what you will be cooking during that week. Use the same guidelines as you would for shopping for staples by first checking to see if you have any of these items already on hand and if so, justify your shopping list by subtracting the amount on hand from the amount needed. You should always have some ready-to-eat snacks to fill in between meals and also for food on the run. When stocking perishable goods, you must take into account their shelf life and don't over stock these items.

For starters, here are some staples that all kitchens should have on hand. You will need to determine how much to stock in your kitchen based upon projected consumption.

Dry Goods

- Flour
- Sugar—white and brown
- Spices
  - **Salt**—kosher for cooking; iodized for baking; sea salt for table salt
  - **Pepper**—white pepper for cooking; black pepper for red meats and table condiment
  - **Granulated garlic**
  - **Dried oregano or Italian seasoning**
  - **Paprika**
  - **Nutmeg**
  - **Cinnamon**
  - **Cumin**
  - **Chili Powder**
- **Oil**—standard vegetable oil for cooking; olive oil for salads
- **Vinegar**—cider vinegar and red wine vinegar
- **Rice**—preferably brown

- Dried pasta
- Canned tomatoes
- Garlic
- Onions—yellow or white for cooking; red for salads
- Potatoes
- Quinoa
- Bread
- Stocks—chicken, beef, vegetable

Refrigerated Goods

- Eggs—preferably organic
- Milk—whichever fat level is good for you; preferably organic
- Orange juice—or other fruit juices
- Bottled water
- Mustard—yellow and Dijon
- Mayonnaise
- Ketchup
- Butter—unsalted for cooking; salted for the table
- Cut fruit
- Carrots
- Lettuce

Frozen Goods

- Shrimp
- Chicken breasts—portioned and vacuum sealed
- Ground beef—portioned and vacuum sealed
- Vegetables not in season—corn, peas
- Other meat—pork, lamb, veal; portioned and vacuum sealed

Snacks

- Fresh fruit—bananas, apples, pears, plums, oranges
- Cheese—low fat in portion sizes
- Yogurt
- Carrot and celery sticks
- Crackers

Additional Items Depending on Use

- Powdered ginger
- Cayenne pepper
- Canned beans
- Pickles
- Old Bay seasoning
- Smoked paprika
- Coffee
- Tea
- Cocoa powder
- Olives—canned or refrigerated
- Asian vegetables—frozen or canned
- Soy sauce
- Tofu
- Canned soup
- Cream or half and half
- Wine for cooking—white (Sauvignon Blanc) and red (Cabernet sauvignon)

Shop for fresh vegetables, meat, and fish as needed. With the exception of frozen shrimp, fish in particular should be purchased on the day you plan to use it.

CHAPTER SIX

Basic Technique

KNIFE SKILLS

In order to maximize the efficiency of your knife and to ensure personal safety, it is important to practice proper knife skills. In Chapter 2 of this book, you learned about the five members of a startup knife kit. In this chapter, we will describe the proper holding techniques for each and the mechanics of safe knife use.

As previously stated, the chef knife is the work horse of the kitchen. It can be used to perform almost any task in the kitchen; however, specific tasks may be more easily done with a specialized knife. The safest and most efficient way to use a chef knife is to do so with knife in constant contact with the cutting board. The knife is held between the thumb and forefinger in a spot on the blade just in front of the bolster. Some knife experts refer to this as the pinch point. The other hand is held against the side of the blade, with the fingers curled and thumb tucked behind.

Chopping & Cutting

The motion in chopping or cutting the product is a smooth slice and chop. All of the cutting is done on the stroke away from the user. When drawing the knife back to reposition, it is lifted by the handle with the tip still in contact with the cutting board and the stroke is repeated. The knife and the hand not holding the knife are moved in unison, progressively chopping the vegetable. **Vegetables are never fed into the knife.** This is a bit dangerous and almost certainly will result in the user's fingers being placed in harm's way.

Since there are no square fruits or vegetables, left to their own device, fruits and vegetables tend to roll on a cutting board. This is not good for safety or accuracy. This being the case, the first priority when processing them is to establish a flat side and place the product on the board on that flat side so that it remains stationary. From that point, the particular cut desired is more easily achieved. For smaller cuts, like mincing, the knife is place horizontally in front of the user with the hand not holding the knife resting on top of the spine. The motion then becomes more of a repetitious chop.

It is obvious that not all fruits and vegetables can be processed by while keeping the knife in contact with the cutting board. Some are just too large to do so. In these cases, the holding technique is with all four fingers wrapped around the handle and the thumb on the spine of the knife. In this scenario, the user has maximum control of the knife and is able to apply maximum pressure in cutting the product. This holding style should be considered only temporary in order to break down the product to the point where the desired holding style can be used.

Paring knives are used for coring, peeling, and fine work like garnishing. Since the invention of the vegetable peeler, their utility has diminished. They are still quite handy, however, for coring. When coring, great caution should be taken not to use the paring knife to gouge the vegetable. This improper technique can easily result in a stab wound to the base of the thumb. Although paring knives are small, the user must maintain the same respect regarding safety as one would when using a larger knife. To properly core a vegetable, the knife is held on the blade in a manner similar to that of holding a Chef knife. This ensures that there is not excessive leeway as one would have if they held it on the handle. Using the tip of the knife, the user pierces the product near the part being removed. The paring knife is then held in place while the vegetable or fruit is rotated with the other hand to finish the core.

Onions Need Special Attention

Onions are perhaps the most widely used vegetable in the American kitchen. Unfortunately, they can be the most problematic to process. They tend to make people cry when processing; they sometimes have a slippery outer layer; and the brown skin is sometimes not uniformly distributed so that when they are peeled, an extra layer may have to be removed. There are many ways to slice or chop an onion. The method described below covers the most number of techniques with a single onion.

Start by coring the stem end of the onion with a paring knife according to the technique previously described. Leave the root end intact. Slice the onion in half longitudinally, by slicing the root in half. Lay both halves on the cutting board, flat side down. To slice one half of the onion, remove the remnants of the root and slice it by way of the technique described earlier in this chapter. Slice in the same direction as the lines on the onion.

To chop the other half of the onion, place that half in front of you with the intact half root furthest from you. Using the tip of the knife to breach the surface, make a series of slices beginning just in front of the root so that the slices are held together by the root. Do not slice the onion completely through the root. Then, holding the knife parallel to the board, make a transverse cut, again stopping short of cutting through the root. Depending on the size of the onion and the size of the desired dice, you may need to make or two more similar cuts. Finish the dice by turning the onion 90° and chopping across the slices to produce chopped onions.

Different Knives for Different Functions

As described in chapter 2, there are three styles of carving, or slicing knives with three different functions A blunt end carving knife is used to carve roasts without a bone. The blade must be wider than the roast being sliced. The knife is held in the same style as when holding a Chef knife when processing large

items. The slicing motion is back and forth so that the blade—not the user—does the cutting. If the knife is properly honed and sharpened, it should require little effort to carve.

The pointed carving knife can be used to carve roasts with or without a bone. It can also be used for repetitive work that one might otherwise use a paring knife for, such as supreming twenty or more oranges. A serrated carving knife is used to slice items that have a hard exterior and a soft interior, such as a tomato or a loaf of bread. This is why they are sometimes referred to as bread knives.

Nomenclature for Various Cuts

In conjunction with learning and practicing knife skills, it is important to learn the names of the various cuts. Like the majority of Western cooking, the nomenclature for these cuts comes from France and French cuisine. You are probably familiar with the common names, like slice and dice. We will define each of them further for you. The procedures and products we will be using are:

- **Concassé**—the verb form of this word, which ends in –er rather than –é, means to chop coarsely. The noun concassé almost always refers to a peeled, seeded, and chopped tomato.
- **Supreme**—the term supreme has several meanings in cooking. With respect to knife skills it refers to any citrus fruit that is segmented, yielding only the edible and palatable portion.
- **Batonnet**—the dimensions of a batonnet are 2 inches by ¼ inch by ¼ inch. This cut is frequently used for zucchini and carrots.
- **Allumette**—also called matchstick. The dimensions of this cut are 2 inches by ⅛ inch by ⅛ inch.
- **Julienne**—You are probably familiar with this word. It is often misused to describe any thin strip cut. Its true dimensions are 2 inches by one-sixteenth inch by one-sixteenth inch.
- **Large dice**—large dice is a cube whose sides are ¾ inch each.
- **Medium dice**—medium dice is a cube whose sides are ½ inch each.
- **Small dice**—small dice is a cube whose sides are ¼ inch each.
- **Brunoise**—the smallest dice, brunoise is a cube whose sides are one-sixteenth inch each. It is usually used as a garnish for consommé.
- **Chiffonade**—a thinly sliced leaf vegetable.
- **Paysanne**—a flat dice that is ½ inch by ½ inch by ¹⁄₁₆ inch.

COOKING TECHNIQUES

Picture this. You're dining in one of Manhattan's most exclusive restaurants. You've just finished your Cognac and you wish to personally compliment the chef. You sneak past the stately maître d' into the kitchen. You pass through the mound of pots and pans in the ware washing area and you find yourself approaching the hot line. The famed Chef Henri has his back to you as he prepares his latest masterpiece. Then you notice that he has a cookbook in one hand and a whisk in the other. You overhear him thinking out loud, "Was that two teaspoons of tarragon or three?" Sound a bit like science fiction? That's because you wouldn't expect a four star chef to rely on a cookbook for his prize-winning recipes. But what is it that separates the professional chef from the home cook when it comes to assembling a recipe or dish? Chefs have been trained to cook by technique. They do, of course get ideas from cookbooks but most times they interpret and execute these recipes in a manner that is consistent with their training. With a general understanding of the classic techniques of French cooking, the home cook can utilize the same knowledge that chefs do in creating and preparing their own recipes.

The process of cooking, as opposed to the field of cooking, can be defined as the transfer of heat to a food product. If we use the branch of science that deals with heat (Thermodynamics) as our guide, we can define each of the techniques of cooking in scientific, thereby unambiguous, terms. Thermodynamics recognizes three forms of heat or heat transfer. They are radiant heat, conductive heat, and convective heat. **Radiant heat** is heat that comes directly from the source, such as the sun, a flame, or a heating element. **Conductive heat** is heat that comes from the source and is transferred to a conductor, then transferred to the product. **Convective heat** is heat that comes from air or liquid that has been heated by the source and circulated. Since there are only three forms of heat transfer and six classic techniques of cooking, some techniques are further differentiated by defining the type of conductor or the type of heat source that is employed.

Poaching

Poaching is defined as a wet technique for cooking light meats, seafood, vegetables, eggs, and various types of forcemeat products. The type of heat that is employed in poaching is conductive heat (and convective heat to a degree). The conductor is an aqueous (water based) liquid, usually water, wine or stock. There are two distinct styles of poaching—shallow poaching and deep poaching. In shallow poaching, small pieces of the product are partially immersed in a poaching liquid and simmered until done. The poaching liquid is then referred to as a *cuisson* and is usually used as a base for a sauce. Deep poaching is a full immersion technique for poaching large, often whole products, such as whole salmon or lobster. The poaching liquid is called *court bouillon*, and is a combination of wine, stock, seasoning vegetables, and herbs. The court bouillon is prepared ahead of time and the product, often served cold, is generally chilled and stored in the court bouillon.

Broiling and Grilling

Broiling can be defined as any high-temperature, dry technique of cooking that employs radiant heat as the primary source of cooking. Until thirty-five or forty years ago, this definition stood on its own merit. With the invention of the microwave, which also employs radiant heat to cook food, it is now necessary to clarify the classic definition of broiling by adding the words "except for microwave cooking." In most cases, the heat source for broiling is either a flame or an electric heating element. The product may be placed under or over the heat source, and in some instances it is placed between two sources of heat so that it is cooked on both sides at the same time. The classic French broiler consists of an overhead flame with a ridged iron tray beneath. The tray rolls in and out of the broiler and the distance from the flame may be adjusted. The tray is usually placed on the closest setting to the flame and heated to very hot before use. The product is then placed on the superheated sliding tray and inserted in the broiler at an appropriate height beneath the flame. This process sears the product on both sides and seals in the juices.

True broiling is meant to be a quick process. The variables that may determine how long this process takes are the distance the product is from the heat source, the type of product, especially the thickness, and the intensity of the heat source. There are a few cooking techniques that are designed to duplicate or enhance the broiling process. **Grilling** is a dry technique of high temperature cooking that produces a product of similar qualities to that of broiling. The product is placed on a hot, ridged surface, usually made of cast iron, and cooked rapidly. Since the type of heat used in grilling is conductive heat, it is not considered to be true broiling, even though it produces favorable results. **Barbecuing** combines flame broiling and smoking with roasting. In its most refined state, the process employs elements of all three techniques, as well as allowing the cook to vary the temperature that the food is exposed to.

The candidates for broiling are premium quality, usually single-serving portions of meat, poultry, fish, and vegetables. The products should be of a thickness that will allow for quick, thorough cooking without burning. Sometimes the product is first marinated to add flavor and to tenderize. Otherwise, dry seasonings or rubs are applied just prior to cooking. If broiling on a grill above the heat source, it is important from an aesthetic point of view to mark the product in what is referred to as a "ten o'clock; two o'clock" pattern. This is a reference to the relative position of the hour hand on a clock at ten o'clock and two o'clock. It means that the product should be seared on the slats or raised portion of the grill or rack to achieve parallel marks that form a diamond shape. This is achieved by first placing the product in a position that would be ten o'clock in relation to the twelve o'clock position of the parallel ridges or slats of the rack. Approximately two to three minutes later the product would then be repositioned to the two o'clock position relative to the ridges or slats. This should produce seared grill marks in the desired diamond pattern.

For many products, the process of broiling allows the diner to choose a degree of doneness that they would like their food cooked to. This is especially true for steaks and chops. The ability to successfully and consistently broil a product to the desired degree of doneness requires the cook to be familiar with the particular broiler setup they are using. They must incorporate all the variables previously mentioned into a formula for success. Testing a product by pressing on the surface with the fingers or a short pair of tongs during the broiling process should verify the degree of doneness. The more a product is cooked, the firmer it will be. Practice will make this procedure more reliable.

Roasting

Roasting is defined as a dry, high-heat, low-heat oven technique of cooking. The type of heat that is employed in roasting is convective heat. This means that the product should be completely surrounded with the hot air that is present in an oven for the technique to work properly. This is usually achieved by placing the product on a rack within or above the roasting pan. Roasting is differentiated from its closest relative, baking in that the conductive heat of the pan is used to transfer heat to the product when baking.

Candidates for roasting are medium to high quality meat and vegetables. The products are usually large and sometimes represent the entire cut of meat or the entire animal. There are some cases in which small pieces of meat are roasted. An example would be the *tandoor* or clay pot cooker that is used in East Indian and Pakistani cooking. Roasting is generally a two-step process with respect to temperature. The sequence of high heat and low heat depends largely on the size and type of product being roasted. Large cuts of red meat are first seared at high temperature, then slow cooked at low heat to ensure tenderness. Pork is usually slow cooked first, then seared with high heat to finish it. This sequence prevents the pork from "bleeding," or losing its natural juices. Larger poultry, such as turkey or goose, are cooked in the same manner. Smaller poultry, like chicken in the two- to three-pound range is cooked by high heat, then low heat. Very small pieces of meat can be roasted with high heat only. This is the case with *Tandoori* items, which are placed on long skewers and then immersed in the 600°F tandoor.

Most roasted items are seasoned liberally before being cooked. This is some-times referred to as "dry rub." The simplest of rubs is coarse ground kosher salt and pepper. Poultry is usually stuffed before roasting. This seasons the product and regulates the heat. Stuffing that is meant to be eaten should be removed from the cavity of poultry and further cooked in a baking dish before serving. Roasted items that need to be portioned or sliced before serving should rest after cooking. This resting period allows the juices to congeal and produces a juicier, more flavorful product. The length of resting time depends on the size of the product, meaning that the larger the product, the longer the resting time. Remember that roasted items will exhibit "carry over cooking" when removed from the oven. Depending on the size of the product, the internal temperature will rise up to approximately five degrees. When the product is removed from the oven, it should be covered with aluminum foil and placed in a warm, not hot, section of the kitchen.

Braising

Braising is defined as a wet technique of cooking that combines sautéing and poaching, in that order. Foods that are suitable for braising are medium to low quality cuts of meat and firm vegetables, such as leeks, celery, and Brussels sprouts. The process tenderizes the product and preserves the flavor. Cuts of beef that are best suited to braising are chuck, round, brisket, and short ribs. Wild game and other less tender cuts of lamb and pork are also candidates for braising. Since it is a two-step procedure that combines two of the other classic techniques of cooking, following the guidelines of each technique will produce the best results.

As in sautéing, meat may be dredged in flour or cooked as is. Start with a very hot pan and a minimal amount of cooking oil or fat. Whole roasts, such as chuck pot roast or beef knuckle may be seared on all sides. Small pieces should be added a few at a time and cooked in small batches so as not to reduce the heat of the sauté pan. It is important to completely sear the product before proceeding to the poaching step. Mirepoix or other seasoning vegetables may be added to the pan and sautéed until caramelized. Choose an appropriate braising liquid, such as beef, chicken or vegetable stock. Wine or spirits may be added to supplement the flavor. As in sautéing, use the liquid to deglaze the pan. Bring to a boil and either return the meat to the same pan or combine all ingredients in a larger pot that is fitted with a lid. The product should be mostly or completely immersed in the braising liquid. Season with any optional seasonings that may be specific to the dish. Return to a boil, cover, and simmer either on top of the stove or in a 350°F oven. The braising time will vary from product to product. Size, shape, and product type are all factors contributing to cooking time. Typical braising time is thirty minutes for vegetables and up to four hours for meat.

Sautéing

Sautéing is defined as a high temperature, dry technique for stovetop cooking. The type of heat that is used to sauté is conductive heat and the conductor is the sauté pan. This differs from sautéing's closest culinary relative, frying, in that the heated oil is the conductor for frying. Since it is the pan itself that is the conductor, only a minimal amount of oil is used to sauté, i.e., only enough oil to keep the product from sticking to the pan.

There are several culinary parameters that are usually associated with sautéing. Small, thin pieces of high quality meat, fish, and vegetables are generally used as starting materials. As previously mentioned, the pan is very hot and only a small amount of oil is used. After the item is sautéed, the pan is usually deglazed with stock, wine, or sauce and a sauce is prepared from that liquid. Items may be dusted lightly with flour before sautéing, but this is not mandatory.

Frying

Frying is defined as an oil-immersion technique of cooking. The type of heat employed in frying is conductive heat and the conductor is the oil. This differs from frying's closest culinary relative, sautéing, in that the conductor for sau-téing is the sauté pan itself. Recognizing this fundamental difference is crucial to understanding the process of cooking. It is important to have enough oil in the fryer or pan to surround the product. To a lesser degree, fried food is also cooked through convective, or circulated heat. Other characteristics of frying that are different from sautéing are: the temperature of the oil is usually medium to medium-high, or approximately 350°F; the product is usually breaded; the pan is almost never deglazed; the product is usually served with a cold sauce instead of a hot sauce; a wider variety of product grades, from low-quality to premium quality may be fried.

With the exception of potatoes, almost all products that are fried are first breaded. The three-step process of breading before frying is referred to as **standard breading procedure.** It starts with a dusting of flour, which dries the exterior and allows the breading to stick. Next, the product is immersed in egg wash, which is a combination of whipped eggs and water, or milk. Finally, the product is dredged in breadcrumbs. Other breadings may be cornmeal, cracker crumbs, shredded potatoes or coconut. Some products may be breaded ahead of time and may also be frozen.

It is very important to preheat the oil before frying. This will prevent the product from absorbing too much of the oil during the cooking process. Choose oil with a high smoke and flash point, such as solid shortening, peanut oil, lard or combination oils. It is easiest and safest to fry in a deep fat fryer, such as the Waring Pro Deep Fryer or DeLonghi Roto Deep Fryer. If not using a deep fryer, you may substitute a wok or frying pan with perpendicular edges, called a *sautoir. Panéing* is a technique of pan-frying that is popular in Cajun cooking. If you are not using an electric deep fryer with thermostatic control, you should monitor the heat of the oil with a reliable thermometer, such as the Taylor candy-jelly-deep fry thermometer. If frying in a stovetop device, such as a wok or sautoir, you should take steps to minimize the inherent fire hazard by having a fire extinguisher handy and also by not overloading or overheating the pan.

Once the oil reaches the proper temperature, carefully immerse the breaded product and cook until GB&D (golden brown and delicious). Measure the internal temperature of meat, poultry and fish to assure the degree of doneness. Larger products may be finished in a 350°F oven to reach the proper internal temperature. If the product appears oily, it may be dried on paper towels before serving. Other than seasoning associated with the breading procedure, all seasonings, such as salt and pepper should be added just prior to serving. Oil may be cooled, strained and reused. Inspect used oil before each use by smelling. Oil used to fry fish should be dedicated to this use.

Barbecuing

One of our nation's favorite pastimes, barbecuing is a method of cooking by which meat, poultry, vegetables, or fish (either whole or in pieces) are covered and slowly cooked in a pit or on a spit, using hot coals or hardwood as a heat source. Most food is first coated with a dry rub of spices and then basted with a mopping sauce once it is on the grill. Barbecuing combines flame broiling and smoking with roasting. In its most refined state, the process employs elements of all three techniques, as well as allowing the cook to vary the temperature that the food is exposed to.

Barbecuing is a term that can cause confusion. In some parts of the country, it signifies a food that has been basted repeatedly with a barbecue sauce during grilling. In others, it refers to pit or spit roasted item. On some menus it may have little if anything to do with either a pit, spit or grill. A barbecued sandwich may simply be roasted beef that has been thinly sliced and simmered in a barbecue sauce.

The two most popular fuel sources for barbecuing are gas and charcoal. Charcoal fires should be started at least thirty minutes prior to cooking time. If you're using a **charcoal grill,** the most efficient way to start the coals is with a chimney starter. Basically a piece of sheet metal that has been molded into a tube whose dimensions are approximately six to eight inches tall by six inches in diameter, the chimney starter is loaded with charcoal and ignited with newspaper kindling. The coals are ready in about twenty to thirty minutes. Coals should always be white before placing items on the grill.

The beauty of using a **gas grill** is the ease of operation, shorter fire-up time and ability to regulate the heat more accurately. Gas grills need only be started up fifteen minutes ahead of cooking time. The downside of gas grills is that with gas alone, the product does not develop the level of smoky flavor that you can get from a charcoal grill. You can offset this effect by using a wood chip box on your gas grill. There are several versions of this piece of equipment, so you should read the manufacturer's instructions for proper use.

For charcoal grills, soak the wood chips in water for thirty minutes, then place directly on white coals. Hardwoods like oak, cherry, pecan, and hickory work best. There are many types of wood chips on the market today, including Sugar Maple and Jack Daniels (from oak aging barrels). Use strong flavored woods like mesquite and hickory for steaks and ribs; fruit tree woods like apple, pecan, and cherry for poultry; and alder wood for fish.

Once the fire is ready, scrape the hot grill surface thoroughly with a stiff wire brush or grill scraper. Some products may be marinated beforehand to add flavor and to tenderize. Otherwise, dry seasonings or rubs are applied just prior to cooking. Spray the product with oil before placing on the grill. For single portion meats such as steaks, it is important from an aesthetic point of view to mark the product in what is referred to as the aforementioned "ten o'clock; two o'clock" pattern. It means that the product should be seared on the slats of the grill to achieve parallel grill marks that form a diamond shape. This is achieved by first placing the product in a position that would be ten o'clock in relation to the twelve o'clock position of the parallel ridges or slats of the grill. Approximately two to three minutes later the product would then be repositioned to the two o'clock position relative to the slats. This should produce seared grill marks in the desired diamond pattern.

Many barbecue grills are equipped with tight fitting lids with adjustable vents and some are large enough to have chimneys, flues, and side compartments for wood. Barbecuing becomes a true art form when these features are used properly. If you have a large, often cylinder-shaped rig, you should start the fire at the end that is not below the chimney. The idea is to have a hot zone and a cool zone so that meat can be manipulated from zone to zone. If you have a side wood compartment, chips or larger pieces of hard wood can be smoldered to enhance flavor. For larger pieces of meat such as brisket, the meat is first seared over the hot side and then moved to the cool side for slow roasting. This process also works to a lesser degree with single serving cuts like steaks. The flue and vents can be manipulated to control the heat and level of smoke. The product should be basted with mopping sauce periodically to preserve moistness.

For some products, the process of grilling allows the diner to choose a degree of doneness that they would like their food cooked to. This is especially true for steaks and chops. Successful, consistent grilling to the desired degree of doneness requires the cook to be familiar with the particular grill setup they are using. They must incorporate all the variables previously mentioned into a formula for success. Practice will make this procedure more reliable. The only fool-proof method for determining the degree of doneness of a grilled product is to take an internal temperature with a reliable meat thermometer.

PART TWO

START WHIPPING THINGS UP

CHAPTER SEVEN

Ten Go-To Dishes to Build Confidence

Since everyone must eat to live, we are all familiar with the art of cooking at some level. This familiarity could be ordering a favorite dish in a restaurant, microwaving a frozen entrée, or attempting new techniques in your home kitchen. Whatever your level of expertise, you should realize that you don't need to be a professional cook to enjoy or excel at the art of cooking. By using a combination of the classic cooking skills covered in Chapter 5, and utilizing the equipment and tools covered in Chapter 2, you can expand your cooking repertoire and increase your comfort level in the kitchen.

In this chapter, we will cover ten "Go-To Dishes" that are easy to prepare and are sure to please. Possibly the easiest bang-for-your-buck dishes are one-pot meals. The "pot" may actually be a roasting or sheet pan, but the format is the same. Here are some examples.

Arroz con Pollo (Mexican-style chicken and rice) **(Serves 4)**

1	whole chicken, about 3–4 lbs., cut into pieces *or* 4 boneless, skinless chicken breasts	1	T. paprika
		1	t. salt
		½	t. black pepper
salt and pepper to taste		3	c. chicken stock
2	T. cooking oil	½	t. dried oregano
2	c. onions, chopped	¼	t. saffron threads
1	green bell pepper, chopped	1	c. frozen peas, unthawed
4	oz. smoked ham, chopped	½	c. roasted pimentos, sliced
2	c. long grain rice	¼	c. green olives, chopped
1	T. garlic, minced		

Season the chicken with salt and pepper and preheat the oil in a large skillet over medium-high heat. Add the chicken and brown well on both sides, about 7 minutes per side. Remove the chicken from the pan and reserve on a plate. Reduce the amount of oil in the pan to 3 tablespoons and add the onions, bell pepper, and smoked ham. Cook about 5 minutes, stirring occasionally. Add the rice and stir to coat with oil. Add the garlic, paprika, salt, and pepper, and cook 1 minute while stirring. Add the chicken stock, oregano, and saffron, and bring to a boil, scraping the bottom of the pan to remove particles. Stir in the chicken, then cover and simmer over medium-low heat for 20 minutes. Stir in the peas, pimentos, and olives; cover and cook until the rice is tender. Taste and adjust seasonings. Serve with green salad for a complete, balanced meal.

German Style Spare Ribs (Serves 4)

1	rack of pork spare ribs	2	garlic cloves, minced
¼	c. cooking oil	12	oz. good German beer
2	t. kosher salt	8	small Yukon Gold potatoes
1	t. black pepper	6	medium carrots, peeled and cut
2	medium onions, sliced		into 2-inch pieces
2	lb. fresh sauerkraut		

Preheat oven to 325°F. Cut the rack of ribs in half. Heat the oil in a Dutch oven over medium-high heat. Season the ribs with salt and pepper, and brown on both sides, one half-rack at a time. Remove and reserve. Add the onions and cook until light brown. Add the sauerkraut with liquid and cook for 10 minutes. Add the garlic and beer and return the ribs to the Dutch oven. Cover the ribs with the sauerkraut mixture and cook 15 minutes, uncovered. Cover and place in a 325° oven for one hour. Add the potatoes and carrots around the rim of the Dutch oven, cover, and cook one hour. Remove the lid and cook an additional 15 minutes.

Italian Style Baked Chicken with Peas, Potatoes, and Carrots (Serves 4)

1	whole chicken, cut into 12 pieces	1	T. salt
6	Russet potatoes, peeled and cut into long wedges	2	t. pepper
		1	T. granulated garlic
4	carrots, sliced	1	T. italian seasoning
2	onions, sliced	2	cans Le Sueur baby peas
¼	c. olive oil		

Preheat oven to 350°F. Place the chicken, potatoes, carrots, and onions in a large bowl and toss with the oil and seasonings. Place in a roasting pan and cook in the oven for an hour, stirring once. Cover with the peas and cook an additional 30 minutes.

SOUPS

Soups can be meals in and of themselves. They generally require only one burner to prepare and, if coupled with bread or dinner roll and possibly a salad, can be a balanced meal.

Clear Soups

Clear soup is one of the three major categories of soup in French cuisine. A clear soup appears on a French menu as *soupe*, generally followed by a series of words that defines the type of clear soup it is. Clear soups in their simplest form are quick and easy to prepare. However, many clear soups involve multiple steps in order to serve them properly. As the name implies, one of the chief criteria for preparing clear soups is that they remain clear. This may sound obvious and simple, but the difficulty lies in the execution. Some components of these soups tend to make the broth cloudy and are therefore better off being prepared separately and added to each individual bowl as needed. Examples of items that fall into this category are starches, dried and cooked legumes, and green, leafy vegetables. Minestrone, for example, is best served by placing cooked pasta, cooked beans, pesto, and spinach chiffonade in each bowl and covering with hot Italian vegetable soup. A clear soup is usually served in a rimless soup bowl or bouillon cup and eaten with a round spoon.

Minestrone (Makes 10 Servings)

¼ c. clarified butter	1 c. tomato, chopped
1 large carrot, diced	2 c. cooked ditalini pasta
1 small onion, diced	2 c. cannelini beans, drained,
1 rib of celery, diced	rinsed, and warmed in a
1 small zucchini, diced	microwave
2 qt. chicken stock	2 c. spinach chiffonade
1 russet potato, diced	4 oz. pesto (recipe follows)
1 c. green beans, cut into ½-inch	
pieces	

Heat the butter over medium heat and sweat the carrots, onion, and celery until soft. Add the zucchini and cook 1 minute. Add the chicken stock and bring to a boil. Add the potatoes and cook 3 minutes. Add the green beans and cook 3 minutes. Add the tomato and remove from the heat. Meanwhile, place 2 tablespoons each of pasta, cannelini beans, spinach, and ½ teaspoon of pesto in each bowl. Pour the hot soup into the bowl. Wait 3 minutes and serve.

This soup can be prepared as a vegetarian soup by replacing the chicken stock with vegetable stock. For a vegan soup, replace butter with olive oil and leave the cheese out of the pesto.

Pesto

4 garlic cloves	½ c. Parmesan cheese, grated
1 c. basil leaves, packed	¼ c. olive oil

Place the first 3 ingredients in a small food processor and process until chopped very finely. Slowly add the oil to form the pesto. Add only enough oil to make a paste. Add more oil if necessary.

Potages

Potages, or thick soups, are one of the three major categories of soup in French cuisine. They would appear on a menu as *Potage* with the description of the type of soup following. Some potages are pureed and may also be strained prior to serving. Dried legumes, like split peas and Navy beans, are often used as bases for thick soups. The dried beans may be soaked in water for several hours before cooking to decrease the preparation time. A basic potage consists of seasoned vegetables, dried legumes, and stock. Many times pork products, such as ham, salt pork, bacon, or ham bones, are used to flavor the soup.

Italian Sausage and Lentil Soup (Makes 8 servings)

This soup is super easy to prepare, is hearty enough to satisfy the appetite, and is sure to be a crowd pleaser. The cooking time can be reduced to 25 minutes by using a pressure cooker. Soaking the lentils in water beforehand can also reduce the cooking time.

1	T. butter, preferably clarified	1	lb. lentils
1	lb. Italian sausage	2	qt. chicken stock
½	c. onions, chopped		salt and white pepper to taste
½	c. carrots, chopped		

Heat the butter in a stockpot. Add the sausage, onions, and carrots, and cook until the sausage is done. Add lentils and toss. Add the stock and bring to a boil. Reduce the heat and simmer for 60 to 90 minutes. Adjust the seasoning with salt and white pepper and serve.

Cream Soups

Cream soups are one of the three major categories of soup in French cuisine. When presented on a French menu, they are called *crème* and generally the description of the soup will follow that word. In American cuisine, many "cream" soups contain no cream at all, but are clear soups thickened with white roux, beurre manié, or corn starch. Traditional French cream soups usually contain a vegetable, seafood, or poultry base, and an appropriate stock. Sometimes starches like rice or pasta are added. They are then finished with cream, usually just prior to serving. A cream soup bowl is shallow and broad, and it's served with an oval soupspoon.

Cream of Leek with Vermicelli Soup (Serves 6–8)

2–3	small leeks	2	qt. chicken stock
¼	c. butter, preferably clarified	½	lb. vermicelli
	salt and white pepper to taste	8–12	oz. cream

This soup is easy to prepare and sure to impress. The base may be made ahead and frozen until ready to use. Leeks are among the most flavorful vegetables a cook can use. However, they are also among the dirtiest. To prepare leeks for cooking, cut off the root and the green tops. Slice the leek longitudinally from top to bottom by making a vertical cut halfway through. Unroll the leek and soak in cold water. Use your hand to rub each layer while immersed in water. Change the water, if necessary. Chop the leeks into ½-inch squares and sweat in clarified butter by cooking until translucent. Season with salt and white pepper. **This is the base.**

Add the chicken stock to the base and bring to a boil. Break the vermicelli into very small pieces that will fit on a soup spoon and boil in the soup until fully cooked. Add the cream, bring to a boil, and remove from heat. Season with salt and white pepper, if necessary. Serve immediately, garnished with paprika.

Cheese and Chive Biscuits (Makes 12 Biscuits)

Here's an easy recipe for biscuits that make a perfect complement to any soup. It does not require the use of a stand mixer or any other equipment. The dough can be made in a standard kitchen bowl and the ingredients can initially be mixed with a wooden spoon. After the initial mixing, the dough is kneaded briefly by hand. The tools required are rolling pin (actually optional—it's that easy), a round cookie cutter the size of the biscuit, and a sheet pan to bake them.

2	c. all-purpose flour	1	stick butter, softened and chopped into small pieces
1	T. baking powder		
½	t. salt	⅔	c. cream or half-and-half
2	T. sugar	½	c. cheddar cheese, grated
		2	T. fresh chives, chopped

Preheat oven to 425°. In a large bowl combine the flour, baking powder, salt, and sugar. Cut the butter into the flour with a wooden spoon or pastry blender, until the butter resembles small peas. Make a well in the center of the mixture and pour the cream in it. With a fork, stir the flour into the cream until the dough is moist. Fold in the cheese and chives. Be careful not to overwork the dough (it doesn't need to hold together well at this point). Let the dough stand for a minute. Lightly flour the work surface and turn dough out onto it. Knead dough 2 or 3 times, until it is holding together and it becomes less sticky. Gently pat the dough to about a ¾-inch thickness and cut the biscuits with a floured cutter. Transfer to a cookie sheet lined with parchment or a Silpat. Bake for 10 to 15 minutes, until risen and golden brown. Place on a wire rack to cool.

SALADS

Salads can also be a complete meal, especially if accompanied by bread or a roll. If you're planning to have a salad as a meal, you should consider including some sort of protein, like chicken, salmon, or quinoa. The best part about salads is that there is generally minimal cooking required. That being the case, extra caution should be taken when handling the ingredients by practicing proper hand washing and possibly wearing food service gloves.

The word salad comes from the Italian word *insalata*, which in turn comes from the Latin phrase *herba salata*, which means, "salted greens." The first reference to such a preparation is found in Roman literature, which mentions a mixture of bitter greens covered with salt and left to marinate; thereby softening and seasoning the greens. While the classic salad is still made largely with greens, salads may be prepared from almost any food group, including vegetables, fruits, meats, fish, grains, and dairy.

There are four basic components to a salad: base, body, dressing, and garnish. Sometimes, one or two of these components are combined before plating the salad, as is the case with fish, meat, and starch salads. Many times the **base** of a plated salad is a lettuce leaf that has been fanned to cover the bottom of the plate. The **body** is generally the major component of the salad and it is often named in this manner (e.g., tuna, potato, and pasta). **Dressings** are often made separately from the salad and either added at the last minute, sometimes "tossing," or placed in a cruet at the table so that each guest can add their own. **Garnishes** may be anything that makes a salad look appealing and may also be incorporated into the body.

Vinaigrettes are a particular type of salad dressing that fall into the category of emulsion dressings. Vinaigrettes are **temporary emulsions**, in that the suspension does not last long; requiring the dressing to be re-emulsified by shaking or stirring before each use. The net effect of forming an emulsion is that the viscosity of the liquid increases. This is particularly evident in the preparation of mayonnaise. Often, an emulsifier, such as lecithin, is added to dressings to assist and prolong the suspension. Egg yolks are particularly high in lecithin and are frequently used for this purpose. Other emulsifiers are mustard and cheese.

To prepare standard vinaigrette, the aqueous or acid portion is placed in a blender or mixer along with any emulsifiers and the organic portion, or oil is slowly added while stirring vigorously. The acid may be vinegar, citrus juice, or soy sauce with a touch of rice wine vinegar or wine. The oil may be any type of your choosing, such as olive, canola, or peanut. The standard ratio is one part acid to three parts oil. You may make low-fat vinaigrette by substituting water for one part of the oil.

Other salad dressings may be made from mayonnaise-type emulsions, dairy products, or combinations of pureed vegetables, herbs, and spices.

Quinoa and Kale Salad with Lemon Vinaigrette (Serves 6)

Dressing:

1 T. Dijon mustard	¾ c. olive oil
1 t. sugar or honey	salt and pepper
¼ c. lemon juice	

Place mustard, honey, and lemon juice in a glass bowl and slowly whisk in oil. Season with salt and pepper.

4 c. kale, cleaned and chopped	1 large English cucumber, diced
1 c. quinoa, cooked	3 T. sunflower kernels, toasted

In a large bowl toss together kale and 2 tablespoons of the lemon dressing. Mix well to coat the leaves (you may also use gloved hands to massage the dressing and kale together). Let it sit for about 2–4 minutes. Add quinoa, cucumber, and sunflower kernels to the kale mixture, mixing everything well. If the salad is dry at this point add about another 2–4 tablespoons of the dressing. Toss everything to coat all the ingredients. Serve salad chilled, garnished with additional sunflower kernels.

Potato, Green Bean, and Cherry Tomato Salad (Serves 6)

1½	lb. slender green beans
2	lb. small red skin potatoes, quartered
3	T. white wine vinegar
8	T. fresh orange juice
1	pt. cherry tomatoes
2	T. Italian parsley, chopped
⅓	c. extra virgin olive oil
6	T. capers

Boil the green beans in a multi-cooker for 5 minutes. Remove, shock in cold water, and reserve. This can be done a day ahead. Boil the potatoes for 8–10 minutes; remove from the multi-cooker and chill under cold running water. Place potatoes in a wooden salad bowl and toss with 2 tablespoons vinegar and 2 tablespoons orange juice. Add green beans, tomatoes, and parsley. Make a dressing by whisking together the remaining vinegar and orange juice and slowly adding the olive oil while whisking vigorously. Fold in the capers. Dress the salad and season with fresh ground black pepper.

> You can boost the protein level of this salad by adding tuna or salmon.

Greek Tomato Salad **(Serves 6–8)**

The beauty of this salad is threefold. It is very easy to make, it makes even hot-house tomatoes taste like tomatoes out of the garden, and the leftover marinade makes an excellent tomato vinaigrette dressing. Start the marination at least four hours prior to serving, or even leave them overnight. Try to use pitted Kalamatas and imported feta.

6–8	beefsteak tomatoes, sliced
¼	c. red wine vinegar, preferably balsamic
¾	c. extra virgin olive oil
1–2	T. kosher salt
1	t. thyme leaves
1	t. coarse ground black pepper
½	t. garlic powder
8	oz. pitted Kalamata olives
8	oz. feta cheese, crumbled

Place the sliced tomatoes in a plastic container with a tight-fitting lid. Add the next 6 ingredients, secure the lid and shake gently to mix. Marinate at least 4 hours. When ready to serve, fan the tomatoes in a circle to cover the outermost portion of a round serving platter. Place the olives in the center and sprinkle the feta over the tomatoes. Garnish with large sprig of basil. Reserve the marinade to use as tomato vinaigrette dressing.

The following recipe is a multi-step recipe for a healthy version of fish wrap with french fries. The "fries" are actually baked after tossing with olive oil, so there is no need to have a deep fryer or a pot of oil for frying. The wrap setup could be used for other items, like chicken.

Fish Fillet Wrap (Makes 6 Servings)

1½ lb. cod, cut into 6 pieces
½   T. sea salt
1   t. paprika
1   t. white pepper
1   t. garlic powder
1   t. Italian seasoning

Mix spice ingredients in a small bowl. Rub the fish pieces with the spice mix; grill to an internal temperature of 150°. Serve as a wrap.

Tzatziki

2   c. plain yogurt
½   English cucumber, grated
2   cloves garlic, minced
3   T. olive oil
1   t. salt

Combine all ingredients in a medium bowl and chill.

Wrap Setup

6   whole wheat tortilla wraps
¼   head iceberg lettuce, shredded
2   tomatoes, chopped
½   English cucumber, chopped
¼   red onion, diced
1   recipe tzatziki

To assemble the wraps:

Place wrap on counter. Add fish and any additional items from the wrap setup. Dress with tzatziki and roll to enclose, folding one end midway through to contain the ingredients. Serve with french fries.

Oven Roasted French "Fries" (Serves 6)

2   lb. Russet potatoes, peeled and cut to french fry size
½   c. olive oil
1   T. sea salt
1   t. white pepper
4   T. garlic powder

Preheat oven to 450°F. Toss all ingredients together in a large bowl. Spread on a sheet pan with a Silpat. Roast at 450°F for 30 minutes, turning once.

CHAPTER EIGHT

Getting a Little Fancier—Six Complete Menus

Now that you are cooking, it's time to add a little bit of panache to your repertoire. Possibly the single most profound difference between restaurant cooking and home cooking is the use of sauces. In this chapter, we'll explore the six "Mother Sauces of French Cuisine" and cover six complete menus. Each menu will incorporate one classic technique of cooking (as described in Chapter 5) and one sauce. Each menu will be a balanced, complete meal with protein, starch, and vegetable. We will also discuss how to utilize any leftovers by converting them to other dishes, thereby saving money and reducing waste.

SAUCES

The first mention of sauce in literature comes from *De re Conquinaria Libri Decem* ("Cuisine in Ten Books"), published in the first century AD by the Latin food connoisseur, Marcus Gavius Apicius, also known as Apicius the Second. He describes a thickened liquid called *granie*, which he used to enhance the flavor of certain seafood. Many historians believe that it was a clerical error in translation that gave us the English word gravy, originally spelled *gravie*. His recipe book was used for centuries after its publication.

During the Renaissance, culinary art experienced the same type of dramatic advances that art in general did, especially in the courts of the royalty in Italy.

Sauce technology and artistry flourished in the court cuisine of Florence and Bologna. In 1535, fifteen-year-old Caterina de Medici, of the ruling family in Florence, went to France to marry the future king, Henri II. Having experienced an enlightened lifestyle, her main concerns were changes in the amenities she had grown accustomed to. Food and diet were of particular concern. The French, at that time, were eating gruel and the fork had not yet been introduced to them. Young Caterina brought her personal chefs with her to France, and this was the spark that spawned Modern French Cooking.

For over 100 years, Italian Renaissance cooking, with all its excesses, dominated the new culinary art of France. In 1651, François Pierre La Varenne published *Le Cuisinier Français*, the first systematic cookbook that chronicled the development of a unique style of cooking in France. This book and three subsequent publications by La Varenne marked the beginning of a new direction in French cooking and also signaled the passing of the torch of Western culinary art from Italy to France. During the eighteenth and early nineteenth century, Marie-Antoine Carême published a series of books that further documented the ingenuity and importance of French culinary art. Primarily a pastry chef, Carême's *L'Art de la Cuisine* listed 186 French sauces and soups and 103 foreign ones.

In 1846, Auguste Escoffier was born in Villeneuve-Loubet, France. Escoffier entered the kitchen at the age of thirteen and began perhaps the most prolific career in the brief history of Modern Western Cuisine, a career that spanned seventy-five years. Escoffier would later become known as "Chef of kings; king of chefs." The German Emperor William II once declared to him, "I am the Emperor of Germany, but you are the Emperor of chefs." Among his many accomplishments, Escoffier opened the Savoy Hotel in London along with Ritz and Echenard, two masters of the hotel business. In 1903, he published *Le Guide Culinaire*, considered by professional chefs to be a treatise on Modern Culinary Art and the Bible of sauce preparation. The English translation of this book is simply called *Escoffier*.

In physics, when two substances that are primarily insoluble in one another are forced into suspension with each other so that they appear and behave as a homogenous mixture, the product is referred to as a **suspension**. When one of these substances is a solid and the other is a liquid, the product is referred to as a solid in liquid suspension, commonly called a **colloidal suspension**. When both substances are liquids, the product is referred to as a liquid in liquid suspension, commonly called an **emulsion**. Physical characteristics of both are similar. The viscosity of the final product is greater than that of the starting materials and the suspension generally has a time limitation. Activation energy, sometimes mechanical, is associated with the formation of both. This activation energy causes the molecules of one of the substances to become completely encircled by the molecules of the other. This, in turn, slows the molecular movement of both, resulting in the corresponding increase in viscosity.

The previous passage is particularly germane to the study of sauces and how they are made. Sauces are defined as thickened, flavored liquids that are applied to food to enhance its flavor. In most cases, this thickening process is achieved through the formation of a suspension. Sauces that are thickened with starch, such as roux, cornstarch, or arrowroot, are colloidal suspensions. Among the Mother Sauces of French cooking, **Velouté, Béchamel, Espagnole** and **Tomàte** are colloidal suspensions. **Hollandaise** and **Mayonnaise** are emulsions.

Starches are long chain molecules, or polymers, comprised of a series of smaller molecules, called monomers or dimers. A more accurate term for starch is polysaccharide. Accordingly, the monomer and dimer units that comprise the long chain starches are called monosaccharides and disaccharides. Both of these smaller units are commonly called sugars. Therefore, one could define a **starch** as a series of sugar molecules bonded into long chains.

Sugar is the primary energy source of all life on earth. When sugar molecules bond together to form a starch, they do so in response to a metabolic need of the plant that they are derived from. In starch form, sugars may be stored within the plant to be used as an energy source at a later date. Two forms of starch that are found in plants are *amylose*, whose sugar units are arranged in a linear, or straight chain fashion, and *amylopectin*, whose sugar units are arranged in a more branched fashion. Generally speaking, grain starches, like cornstarch and flour are high in amylose and tuber starches, like arrowroot and potato starch are high in amylopectin. Studies to determine the relative thickening capacities of each type are inconclusive. Common starches that are used as thickening agents in cooking are flour, cornstarch, arrowroot, tapioca, potato starch, and rice flour. Generally, these starches are combined with liquid and agitated to form a *slurry* prior to use.

Flour is often combined with butter or oil and then cooked to form roux. The cooking process tends to reduce the grainy, or starchy flavor. The length of time the roux is cooked determines the type of roux and its thickening capacity. The **three types of roux** used in French cooking are **white, blonde,** and **brown.** White roux is cooked for only five minutes or less. It retains its white color and is therefore best suited for use in white or light colored sauces. Blonde roux is cooked for five to ten minutes. It has a light brown color and slightly nutty aroma and flavor. It is best suited for light brown or non-white sauces, like Velouté. Brown roux is cooked for up to thirty minutes, often in the oven. It has a dark brown color and a pronounced nutty aroma and flavor. It is best suited for use in dark sauces, particularly Sauce Espagnole. As roux gets darker, its thickening capacity decreases, due to decomposition of the starch.

Roux is approximately 60 percent flour and 40 percent clarified butter or oil, cooked to remove the grainy taste. To make a roux, it is not necessary to measure out the ingredients. Begin by heating the clarified butter or oil in a sauté pan. Slowly add the flour while stirring with a wooden spoon. Add enough flour to produce a consistency equivalent to that of wet sand at low tide. Reduce the heat to medium and cook to produce the desired color.

Clarified butter is used to make roux and sauces as well as for sautéing. Unlike whole butter, clarified butter does not burn at high temperatures. The composition of whole butter is 80 percent butterfat, 18 percent water, and 2 percent milk solids. To prepare clarified butter from whole butter, the water and milk solids are removed, yielding a product that should be close to 100 percent butterfat. To achieve this, slowly melt the whole butter; skim the milk solids off the top; then carefully decant the top layer through a fine strainer or cheesecloth. Be sure not to allow the bottom layer of water and residual milk solids to pass through the strainer.

Brown Sauce Espagnole

Brown Sauce Espagnole is one of the six "Mother Sauces" of French cooking. All classic sauces are derived from one of these. Sauces that use a Mother Sauce as their base are referred to as **"small sauces"** or **"compound sauces."** Examples of small sauces that are derived from Brown Sauce are Sauce Chasseur, Sauce Robert, Sauce Charcuterie, and Sauce Bordelaise. A true Brown Sauce is made with brown veal stock. At least two methods of preparation are in use today. The first method involves making a brown roux prior to starting the sauce and adding it to thicken. In the second method, the roux is made *in situ*, or in the same pot as the sauce.

Velouté Sauce

Velouté Sauce is one of the simplest of the six Mother Sauces of French cuisine. It is stock or broth that is thickened with roux. The sauce is usually named according to the type of stock that is used, e.g., Chicken Velouté, Seafood Velouté, etc. Many times, optional ingredients are added or herbs and other flavorings are infused into the stock prior to adding the roux. Some soups are thin versions of Velouté Sauce.

Sauce Béchamel

Sauce Béchamel owes its name to Louis de Béchameil, Marquis of Nointel, who became major domo to Louis XIV. Born in 1603, Béchameil was rich, an informed art critic and one of the first gourmets, advisers to royalty on matters of culinary art. The sauce itself was already in existence when one of the king's cooks devised a new recipe and named it after Béchameil. The spelling has since changed to its current Béchamel. It is one of the six Mother Sauces of French cuisine. It usually accompanies lighter dishes of seafood, chicken, or eggs. Sauce Soubise, which is Béchamel with sautéed onions, is used to gratiné red meats, thereby being the exception in application. There are two methods for preparing and thickening Sauce Béchamel. The first uses roux as the thickening agent, while the second uses a *liaison* of cream and egg yolks.

Sauce Tomàte

Sauce Tomàte is a French version of Italian spaghetti sauce. It has obvious New World roots and, unlike Italian tomato sauce, uses roux as a thickening agent. An alternative to Sauce Tomàte could be a very straightforward spaghetti sauce that is milled.

Emulsion Sauces

Emulsion sauces are prepared by forcing an aqueous (water-soluble) substance, usually acidic, into an organic (fat or oil based) substance. This process is generally achieved by adding mechanical energy, in the form of vigorous agitation, to the system. There are three types of emulsions. A **temporary emulsion** lasts a very brief time and the product is usually re-emulsified by shaking or stirring just prior to use. An example of a temporary emulsion is a vinaigrette dressing. A **semi-permanent emulsion** is one that lasts for a longer period of time and is usually broken by temperature change. An example of a semi-permanent emulsion is Hollandaise Sauce. A **permanent emulsion** is one that resists breaking, even with temperature changes, and lasts virtually the lifetime of the product. An example of a permanent emulsion is mayonnaise.

Most emulsion sauces begin with a small amount of acidic liquid, sometimes a reduction of vinegar, wine, citrus juices or a combination. Fat or oil, sometimes melted clarified butter or vegetable oil, is then slowly added while vigorously stirring. The rate of addition is critical to achieving the emulsion. If the fat or oil is added too quickly or the stirring is not vigorous enough, the sauce will break, or separate into its component parts. This will be apparent in the appearance and also in the viscosity, which will be relatively unchanged. Emulsifying agents are sometimes added to assist in the formation of the emulsion. Lecithin is one of the most widely used emulsifying agents in food applications. A common source of lecithin is egg yolk. Other emulsifying agents include mustard and cheese.

Hollandaise Sauce
Hollandaise Sauce was invented by the Huguenots while in religious exile in Holland. It is used primarily as an accompaniment to light meats, seafood, vegetables, and eggs. The sauce is made in three stages. First stage is to prepare a reduction. Second stage is to prepare a sabayon by whisking egg yolks into the reduction while gently heating. Third stage is to prepare the emulsion by slowly whisking the butter into the sabayon while maintaining a very gentle, warm temperature.

Mayonnaise
There are several versions of the origins of mayonnaise. One of the most popular ones is that it was invented in the town of Mahon in Spain and then brought to France. A second version is that it was invented in France and is named after the French word for egg yolk. Either way, it is the newest member of the Mother Sauce family and is a cold version of Hollandaise. Oil is substituted for butter in the preparation.

Menu 1
(Serves 8)

Sautéed Medallions of Chicken

---

16 boneless chicken tenders
4   T. clarified butter
salt and white pepper to taste
1   recipe Rosemary Lemon Velouté Sauce (see below)

Lightly pound the chicken tenders with a meat mallet to form thin medallions. Preheat a large sauté pan and add half the butter. When butter begins to smoke, season the medallions with salt and white pepper and quickly sauté. Sauté the remaining medallions in batches, adding more butter as needed. Reserve the cooked chicken on a hot plate. Deglaze the pan with Velouté Sauce. Bring to a boil and serve with chicken.

Rosemary Lemon Velouté Sauce

---

1   qt. chicken stock
1   small sprig fresh rosemary
3–4 oz. blonde roux, cooled to room temperature (Page 123)
juice of one lemon
salt and white pepper to taste

Bring the chicken stock and rosemary to a boil and simmer five minutes. Remove the rosemary, return the liquid to a boil and add the roux in small amounts while whisking. When you reach the proper consistency, lower the heat and simmer for 20–30 minutes. Strain through chinois or fine China cap and finish with lemon juice. Season with salt and white pepper.

Oven Roasted Potatoes

---

8   large Russet potatoes, peeled and sliced into steak fries
salt, white pepper, and garlic powder to taste
⅓ c. olive oil

Preheat oven to 400° F. Place the potatoes in a large roasting pan. Season with salt, pepper, and garlic powder. Toss with olive oil and place in a 400°F oven for 35–45 minutes, turning the potatoes once or twice.

Sautéed Baby Spinach

---

3   lb. baby spinach, cleaned
2   T. clarified butter
1   large shallot, minced
salt and white pepper to taste

Rinse thoroughly and dry spinach in a lettuce spinner. Heat the butter to very hot in a large sauté pan or rondeau. Add the shallot, then the spinach. Season lightly with salt and white pepper, tossing the spinach in the hot pan until cooked.

Glazed Carrots

---

8   carrots, sliced into ½-inch rounds
4   T. whole butter
¼ c. brown sugar
salt and white pepper to taste

Boil the carrots in salted water, drain, and reserve. In a small saucepot, melt the butter and add the brown sugar. Cook to dissolve. Add the carrots and toss, seasoning with salt and white pepper.

What to do with the Leftovers

With any leftover chicken, make the following chicken salad for sandwiches.

2   c. chicken, chopped
¼   c. onion, chopped
¼   c. celery, chopped
½   c. mayonnaise
2   t. curry powder (optional)
¼   c. chopped walnuts (optional)
¼   c. raisins (optional)
salt and white pepper to taste

Place all ingredients in a bowl and mix well.

With any leftover potatoes, make home fries for breakfast.

2   T. oil
2   v. potatoes, chopped
½   c. onion, chopped
salt and pepper to taste
paprika for garnish

Heat oil over medium-high heat. Add potatoes and onions and cook until light brown. Season and serve.

Menu 2

Poached Sole Vin Blanc **(Serves 8)**

This is one of the classic recipes of French cuisine. It may be prepared from true Dover sole, lemon sole, flounder, grey sole, or any very light, white-meat fish that is filleted. The *cuisson*, or residual poaching liquid, is used as the base for the Vin Blanc. Ask your fishmonger to filet the whole fish for you.

8 filets Dover sole, about 5–6 oz. each	½ c. dry white wine
2 T. clarified butter	1 c. fish stock
1 shallot, finely chopped	1 c. thick Béchamel sauce (recipe follows)

Preheat oven to 350° F. Fold the filets in thirds, with the skin side in. Butter the bottom of a sauté pan and add the shallots. Place the filets in the pan and add enough liquid to cover ⅔ of the height of the fish. Bring the pan to a boil on top of the stove, cover with buttered parchment paper, and place in the oven for 8–10 minutes.

Remove from oven and strain the majority of the liquid to a saucepot. Leave the filets in a small amount of the liquid, covered and in a warm place in the kitchen. Bring the cuisson to a boil and thicken with the Béchamel. Strain through China cap or Chinois. Serve the filets with rice pilaf and the Vin Blanc.

Thick Sauce Béchamel **(Yields One Quart)**

6 T. butter, preferably clarified	1 qt. half-and-half or heavy cream
⅓ c. onions, chopped	½ t. fresh ground nutmeg
6 T. flour	salt and white pepper to taste

In a small saucepot, melt the butter and sweat the onions by cooking until translucent. Add the flour and cook slowly for five minutes. Add the half-and-half, stirring constantly with a whisk. Bring to a boil, add the nutmeg; turn the

Continued . . .

heat down and simmer 20–30 minutes. Season to taste with salt and white pepper and strain through Chinois or China cap. Save any unused Béchamel for a future dish (this sauce can be frozen).

Rice Pilaf (Serves 4)

1 T. clarified butter	2 c. stock or water
½ shallot, minced	salt and white pepper to taste
1 c. long grain rice	

Preheat oven to 350° F. Heat the butter in a small saucepot. Add the shallot and cook one minute. Add the rice and stir to coat with butter. Add the liquid and season with salt and white pepper. Bring to a boil, cover, and place in the oven for 17 minutes. Remove, fluff with a fork, and serve.

Baked Butternut Squash (Serves 6–12)

1 butternut squash, cut in half longitudinally and seeded	¼ c. honey
2 T. clarified butter	1 t. nutmeg
	salt and white pepper to taste

Preheat oven to 350° F. Place the squash on a sheet pan, elevated with a crown made of aluminum foil. Cover the bottom of the pan with water. Brush the squash with butter, drizzle with honey, and season with nutmeg, salt, and pepper. Place in oven for 1–2 hours, until tender. Slice into U-shaped strips and serve.

Steamed Asparagus Spears

24–32 asparagus spears

Choose tender spears; trim the root end so that all the spears are the same length. Stand the spears up in a narrow pot of boiling, salted water. Steam for 5–8 minutes, depending on the thickness of the spears. Remove, brush with butter, and serve.

What to do with the Leftovers

Convert the leftover squash to a soup.

2 c. cooked butternut squash	½ c. evaporated milk
1½ c. vegetable stock	toasted pecans for garnish

Preheat the oven to 350°F. Spread the pecans on a sheet pan and toast for 3–5 minutes. Heat the squash, vegetable stock, and evaporated milk in a saucepot over medium heat. Puree with a stick blender or **carefully puree in a standard blender.** (Hot liquids can expand in a standard blender and sometimes escape the vessel, causing burns.) Serve hot, garnished with toasted pecans.

Make a fish mousse with the leftover fish and Vin Blanc.

2 fish filets	½ t. salt
¼ c. Vin Blanc sauce	¼ t. white pepper

Place the fish in a small food processor and puree while slowly adding the Vin Blanc to form a mousse. Add salt and pepper. Serve cold on crackers as an hors d'oeuvre, garnished with gherkin sliver.

Menu 3

Hungarian Beef Goulash (Serves 6–8)

---

4 lb. Trimmed beef chuck, cut into ½-inch cubes
oil or lard for sautéing
4 medium onions, sliced
4 cloves of garlic, minced
zest of two lemons
2 T. cider vinegar
3 T. tomato paste
¼ c. paprika, mild or a mixture of mild and hot
salt and white pepper to taste
2 qt. beef stock
cornstarch slurry to thicken*

Preheat oven to 350° F. In a large braising pan or frying pan, sear the meat in the fat in small batches. Remove and reserve. Add the onions and caramelize. Add the garlic and cook 30 seconds. Add the remaining ingredients, **except the cornstarch slurry.** Return the meat to the pan and bring the mixture to a boil. Reduce to a simmer, and cook in the oven for 2 hours. Test for tenderness after two hours and cook an additional hour if not tender. Remove from oven and place on a burner on top of the stove. Remove the lid, bring to a boil, and thicken with cornstarch slurry. Serve over spaetzle.

*Make a cornstarch slurry by whisking together 3 tablespoons cornstarch and ¼ cup water or beef stock and immediately adding to boiling liquid.

Spaetzle (Serves 6)

Spaetzle are German egg dumplings that are often served as a side dish with Goulash. You can use either water or milk, but milk is preferred. This version also adds a bit of nutmeg.

1½	c. flour	pinch of nutmeg
½	t. baking powder	2 eggs
¾	t. salt	½ c. milk

Combine the dry ingredients. Beat the egg with the milk. Add the wet ingredients to the dry ingredients and mix to form a sticky dough. Bring a large pot of water to a boil. Using a spaetzle maker or potato ricer, drop small dumplings into the water and cook until they float. Drain and toss with butter and a small amount of nutmeg.

Sauce Tomàte (Yields 1½ Quarts)

1	lb. pork neck bones	1	T. salt
2	T. cooking oil	1	T. sugar
2	medium onions, diced	½	t. red pepper
3	cloves garlic, minced	1	t. oregano
2	qt. tomato puree	2	qz. blonde roux

Sear the pork bones in the oil and remove. Sauté the onions until translucent. Add the garlic and cook 30 seconds. Add the puree, spices, and reserved bones, bring to a boil, reduce the heat and simmer for 30 minutes to an hour. Remove the pork bones. Pass through a food mill, return to the saucepot, and bring to a boil. Thicken with blonde roux and serve.

Zucchini Parmagiana (Serves 6–8)

3–4 zucchini	2–3 eggs
½ c. flour	½ c. parmesan cheese
1 t. salt	oil for frying
½ t. white pepper	Sauce tomàte (previous page)
1 t. garlic powder	

Preheat oven to 350° F. Slice the zucchini into 1/4-inch thick circles. Combine the flour, salt, pepper, and garlic powder. Beat the eggs. Heat the oil to medium-high heat. Dredge the zucchini in the flour mixture, then the egg. Fry to GB&D (golden brown and delicious). Cover with cheese and tomato sauce and place in oven for 20–30 minutes.

What to do with the Leftovers

Make four mini beef pot pies with leftover goulash.

½ recipe biscuit dough	½ c. frozen peas
3 carrot sticks, diced	4 premade mini pie shells
2 c. goulash	

Preheat oven to 350°F. Make a batch of biscuit dough (pg. 112). Boil the carrots for 5 minutes. Mix the goulash and carrots with the frozen peas. Place in the pie shells. Roll out some biscuit dough and cover each pie. Cut a few slits in the top. Bake on a cookie sheet for 30 minutes.

Make open faced sandwiches with the leftover zucchini.

4   slices country bread, lightly toasted
enough zucchini parmigiana to cover the slices
½   c. shredded mozzarella

Preheat oven to 350° F. Lightly toast the bread. Top with zucchini and mozzarella cheese. Bake for 12 minutes.

Menu 4

Oven Roasted Chicken (Serves 4)

1	frying chicken, about 3 lbs.	1	rib celery
1	apple		kosher salt and pepper
1	large carrot	⅓	c. flour
1	large onion	2	qt. chicken stock

Preheat oven to 475°F. Remove the gizzards, liver, and neck from the cavity of the chicken. Place an apple in the cavity. Truss the chicken by inserting the legs into two slits in the skin, one on each side. Fold the wing under the chicken. Make a natural rack by slicing the carrot, onion, and celery into thick slices, placing the slices on the bottom of the roasting pan, and placing the chicken on top of the rack. Season with salt and pepper. Cook the chicken for 30–40 minutes at 475°, then lower the temperature to 300° and cook to an internal temperature of 170°, taken in the thigh. Remove the chicken from the oven and allow to rest 20–30 minutes. Make the gravy by placing the roasting pan on top of two burners of the range and adding the flour to form a roux. Cook over medium heat for 3 minutes while whisking. Add the chicken stock and bring to a boil while whisking. If the gravy is too thick, add more stock to thin. If the gravy is too thin, thicken further by adding a cornstarch slurry to the boiling gravy while whisking. Strain the gravy and season with salt and white pepper.

Duchess Potatoes (Serves 6)

2	lb. Russet potatoes, peeled and cut into one-inch cubes	2–3	egg yolks
			salt and white pepper to taste
4	T. whole butter		egg wash

Preheat oven to 350° F. Slowly boil the potatoes in salted water until just done. Strain and place on a sheet pan in a 350°F oven for 4–5 minutes to dry. Remove and process through a potato ricer or food mill. Add the butter, egg yolks, salt, and pepper, and whip with a wooden spoon. Place in a pastry bag with a large star tip and extrude onto a sheet pan with a Silpat to form 1½-inch wide, 3-inch tall "trees." Brush with egg wash and place in a 350°F oven until slightly browned.

Steamed Vegetable Medley **(Serves 6)**

6 carrots, peeled and sliced into "coins"	1 head broccoli, florets only
1 head cauliflower, florets only	4 T. whole butter salt and white pepper to taste

Bring 8 quarts salted water to a boil. Add the carrots, bring back to a boil, and cook 5 minutes. Add the cauliflower and cook five minutes. Add the broccoli and cook 7 minutes. Strain; add the butter, and season with salt and pepper.

Brown Sauce Espagnole

¼ c. clarified butter	1 T. tomato paste or other tomato
½ c. onion, chopped	product
¼ c. carrot, chopped	¼ c. flour
¼ c. celery, chopped	32 oz. beef stock
¼ c. turnip, chopped (optional)	1 bouquet garni of bay leaf and
¼ c. mushroom stems, chopped	thyme (a small piece of celery with
1 T. garlic, chopped	the bay leaf and thyme secured to
1 T. parsley stems, chopped	it with it butcher's twine)

In a 3-quart saucepot, heat the butter to hot. Add the onion, carrot, and celery, and sauté until light brown. Add the turnip and mushroom stems and sauté until the onions and carrots are thoroughly caramelized and dark brown. Add the garlic and parsley stems and cook to aroma, about 30 seconds. Add the tomato product and cook an additional 30 seconds. Add the flour and make a brown roux the consistency of wet sand at low tide. You should lower the heat to make the roux and cook for at least ten minutes. Add the beef stock and bring to a boil. Add the bouquet garni, lower the heat and simmer for at least 2 hours. During this time, you will need to skim the material from the top every 20–30 minutes. Strain through fine China cap or chinois. Season with salt and white pepper.

What to do with the Leftovers

With the vegetables, make timbales.

6 eggs	¼ c. parsley, chopped
3 c. vegetables, pureed	⅔ c. swiss cheese, grated
⅔ c. panko bread crumbs	⅔ c. heavy cream
3 T. onion, grated	salt and white pepper to taste
¼ c. parmigiana cheese	

Preheat oven to 350° F. Start a pot of boiling water for the water bath. Beat the eggs and fold in the remaining ingredients. Butter six 4-oz. ramekins and fill them with the mixture. Place the ramekins in a deep roasting pan and place in the oven. Pour the boiling water into the roasting pan to about ⅓ of the way up the sides of the ramekins. Bake for 20 minutes; then test for doneness by inserting a toothpick. It should come out clean. Invert on plate to remove or serve in the ramekin.

Convert the leftover potatoes to croquettes. (Serves 4)

2 c. Duchess potatoes	1 egg, whipped
½ c. flour	½ c. panko bread crumbs

Preheat a deep fryer to 350° F. Roll the potatoes into ¾-inch logs and cut to 2-inch pieces. Dredge in flour, then egg, then Panko bread crumbs, and fry.

Menu 5

Fried Butterfly Shrimp **(Serves 6–8)**

2 lb. shrimp (16–20 count)	2 eggs
1 t. salt	water for egg wash
¼ t. white pepper	½ c. panko bread crumbs
½ c. flour	oil for frying

Preheat the oil to 350° F in a deep fryer. Peel, devein, and butterfly the shrimp, leaving the tails intact. Combine the salt, white pepper, and flour, and place in a large Ziploc bag. Beat the eggs with water and place in a small bowl. Place the breadcrumbs in a large Ziploc bag. When the oil reaches temperature, put the shrimp in the bag with the flour mixture and shake. Remove and dip into the eggs. Place in the bag with the breadcrumbs, toss, remove, and add to the hot oil. This entire breading procedure may also be done ahead and the shrimp may be stored on parchment paper on a sheet pan. Cook for 2–3 minutes, remove, drain on a paper towel, and serve with Sauce Remoulade (Recipe follows).

French Fried Potatoes **(Serves 4)**

French fries are actually of Belgian origin. American doughboys, however, had their first taste of them while pulling duty in France during World War I. When they returned to the States, they brought with them memories, and hence the demand for "french fries."

4 russet potatoes, peeled
salt and black pepper to taste
oil for frying

Heat the oil to 350° F in a deep fryer. Pass the peeled potatoes through a french fry cutter or cut by hand. Heat the oil to 350°F. Dry the potatoes in a salad spinner and pat dry with paper towels. Cook in batches in the hot oil and keep warm in a 200°F oven. Season with salt and black pepper just prior to serving. Many devotees of true Belgian Fried Potatoes believe that they should be fried twice.

Cole Slaw (Serves 8)

1 small head cabbage	1 c. mayonnaise
2 carrots, peeled and cut into 2-inch	¼ c. heavy cream
pieces	2 T. brown sugar
½ medium red onion, peeled and	2 T. cider vinegar
quartered	salt and Tabasco to taste

Remove the core from the cabbage and cut into 2-inch pieces. Shred the cabbage, carrots, and onion in a food processor. Place in a large wooden bowl and mix thoroughly. Make the dressing by combining the mayonnaise, cream, brown sugar, vinegar, and Tabasco in a bowl and whisking until the sugar is dissolved. Add more mayonnaise if the mixture is too loose, too sweet, or too tart. Add half the dressing to the vegetables and toss. Add the rest, if necessary. Season with salt.

Chilled Beets with Mint (Serves 6)

6 fresh beets	¼ c. fresh mint, chopped
¼ c. vegetable oil	salt and white pepper to taste
2 T. cider Vinegar	

Trim the stems and roots and thoroughly wash the beets. Place in salted water and boil, skins on, until fork tender. This should take 45 minutes to an hour. Remove, drain, and cool under running water. **Reserve the cooking water to make pickled eggs.** Once cool, peel the skins by rubbing with a paper towel. Slice and dress with the oil, vinegar, mint, salt, and pepper. These are better the next day.

Sauce Remoulade

1 c. mayonnaise (recipe follows)	2 T. capers
1 T. shallot, chopped	1 boiled egg, chopped
½ t. Tabasco	1 T. Dijon mustard
1 t. Worcestershire sauce	1 T. fresh lemon juice

Place all ingredients in a small bowl and mix well.

Mayonnaise

2   egg yolks
2   T. cider vinegar
1   c. vegetable oil
salt and white pepper to taste

Add the egg yolks and vinegar to a blender and thoroughly combine. While the blender is on slowly add the oil, until a thick emulsion is formed. Season with salt and white pepper.

What to do with the Leftovers

Make pickled eggs with the leftover beets and reserved cooking water. (Makes 18 Pickled Eggs)

1½ c. brown sugar	6 whole cloves
6 c. beet water (water leftover from cooking the beets)	3 cinnamon sticks
	leftover beets
3 c. vinegar	18 boiled eggs, shelled

Place the brown sugar, reserved beet water, vinegar, cloves, and cinnamon in a saucepot and boil for 10 minutes. Cool and add the beets and eggs. Pickle for 2–3 days.

Menu 6

Broiled Lamb Chops (Serves 4)

8 rib or loin lamb chops, trimmed
olive oil for rubbing
coarse salt and black pepper

Preheat the broiler. Rub the chops with olive oil and season with salt and pepper. Place under or over the broiler. If over a flame, place the product at ten o'clock relative to the rack slats. Two minutes later, place the chops in the two o'clock position. Turn the chops after 4 minutes and cook an additional 4 minutes on the other side for medium to medium-rare. If using double cut chops, broil an additional 2 minutes per side. Remove and serve with Sauce Béarnaise.

Mushroom Risotto (Serves 4)

12 oz. fresh mushrooms, sliced	1 c. arborio rice
6 T. butter	salt and white pepper to taste
salt and white pepper to taste	¼ c. Parmesan, grated
3 c. chicken stock	

Sauté the mushrooms thoroughly in two tablespoons of butter. Season with salt and white pepper and set aside. Heat the stock to almost boiling. In a small saucepot, heat 2 tablespoons butter and add the rice. Cook while stirring for 2 minutes. Add 1 cup of the stock and cook while stirring until it is almost completely absorbed. Repeat this process with the other two cups of stock, cooking until the rice is tender. You may need less or more stock. Season with salt and white pepper. Stir in the last 2 tablespoons of butter, the cheese, and the mushrooms.

Sautéed Zucchini, Yellow Squash, and Red Peppers

2	zucchini	¼	c. butter, preferably clarified
2	yellow squash		salt and white pepper to taste
1	red pepper		

Cut the zucchini and yellow squash into batonnets. Slice the pepper into 1/4-inch strips. Sauté over high heat in the butter and season with salt and white pepper.

Sauce Béarnaise

Sauce Béarnaise is used primarily as an accompaniment to grilled red meat, especially fillet mignon or chateaubriand. It is actually not one of the six Mother Sauces. The preparation is, however, almost identical to that of Hollandaise, the Mother Sauce from which it is derived. The difference between the two is the addition of tarragon in the making of Béarnaise, both in the initial reduction and to finish. The sauce is made in three stages. First stage is to prepare a reduction. Second stage is to prepare a sabayon by whisking egg yolks into the reduction while gently heating. Third stage is to prepare the emulsion by slowly whisking the butter into the sabayon while maintaining a very gentle, warm temperature.

¼	c. white wine vinegar	3	egg yolks
12	black peppercorns	1	pt. clarified butter
1	T. shallot, chopped		dash of Tabasco
3	T. fresh tarragon, chopped		pinch of salt

Prepare a reduction by slowly boiling the vinegar, peppercorns, shallot, and 1 tablespoon tarragon until it is near dryness. Reconstitute with 2 tablespoons water and strain into a small metal bowl. Place the bowl over a pot of nearly boiling water and prepare a sabayon by adding the egg yolks and whisking until creamy and thick. Prepare the emulsion by slowly whisking in the melted, clarified butter. Be careful not to add the butter too fast and not to overheat. You may have to remove the bowl from the double boiler. You may also need to thin the sauce with a small amount of water or vinegar. Finish the sauce with the other 2 tablespoons tarragon, a dash of Tabasco, and salt to taste.

What to do with the Leftovers

Convert the leftover rice and vegetables to a lunch casserole.

2 c. risotto	2 T. butter
2 c. mixed vegetables	½ c. cheddar cheese
½ c. panko bread crumbs	

Preheat oven to 350°F. Mix the risotto and vegetables. Toss the bread crumbs with the butter and coat the bottom and sides of a casserole dish. Add the risotto/vegetable mix and top with cheese and remaining bread crumbs. Bake for 25 minutes and serve.

One Extra Menu for Vegetarians

Baked Tomato Stuffed with Sautéed Spinach and Feta Cheese (Serves 6)

6 ripe tomatoes	½ t. kosher salt
2 T. extra-virgin olive oil	¼ t. white pepper
1 clove of garlic, minced	¼ lb. feta cheese, crumbled
16 oz. fresh baby spinach	

Preheat oven to 350° F. Carefully core the stem end of the tomatoes and score the blossom end with an "x." Place in a pot of boiling water for 15–30 seconds. Remove and shock in ice water. Peel the skin off each tomato and remove seeds and most of the pulp with a melon scoop. Heat the olive oil in a sauté pan over medium-high heat. Add the garlic and spinach and cook until thoroughly sautéed, seasoning with salt and white pepper. Drain well and chop. Cool and mix in the feta. Stuff each tomato with the spinach mixture and bake for 15 minutes. Serve over smoked corn, black beans, and red peppers.

Smoked Corn, Black Beans, and Red Peppers (Serves 6)

In the vernacular of Southwestern cuisine, this mixture is referred to as "mud." It shows up in a variety of dishes, including soups, salads, and entrees.

1 c. black beans	1 Anaheim, cubanelle, or poblano
3 ears corn	pepper (optional)
2 T. clarified butter or canola oil	1 t. kosher salt
1 red bell pepper, medium dice	1 T. chili powder, like Mexene

If cooking dried beans, place one-pound of beans in a large bowl and cover completely with water so that there is at least an inch of water over top. Soak overnight in the refrigerator. Drain and cook slowly in 2 quarts water, seasoning

Continued . . .

with 2 cloves of garlic. Cook until tender, about 2 hours. Add more water as needed. If using canned beans, drain and rinse the beans.

Smoke the corn over apple wood in a Camerons stovetop smoker or on an outdoor grill with smoker box or wood about 15 minutes. Cool and remove the kernels.

In a large sautoir or rondeau, heat the oil or butter over medium heat and cook the peppers until shiny and translucent. Add the beans and corn and toss to thoroughly heat. Season with salt and chili powder. Cover the bottom of six dinner plates with the bean mixture and top with the stuffed tomato.

What to Do with the Leftovers

Convert the "mud" to a Southwestern style soup or a salad. (Serves 4)

1	qt. chicken stock
1	c. smoked corn, black beans, and peppers
4	avocado slices
8	tortilla chips
¼	c. chopped cilantro

Heat the chicken stock to a boil and add the smoked corn, black beans, and peppers. Simmer 5 minutes and serve, garnished with avocado slices, tortilla chips, and cilantro.

Southwestern Style Salad (Serves 4)

1 head iceberg lettuce, chopped	¼ red onion, chopped
1½ c. smoked corn black beans and peppers	juice of 2 limes
	¼ c. chopped cilantro
1 tomato, chopped	salt and pepper to taste
1 avocado, chopped	

Mix all ingredients together and season with salt and pepper.

PART THREE

STEPPING IT UP

CHAPTER NINE

Plating, Presentation, Table Settings, and Service

Plating

Plating is the first step to achieving restaurant quality presentation. Varying the shape, size, and color of the components of the dish is an integral part of plating. Most contemporary American plating is center-based and tall. A plate is like a painter's canvas. The rim of the plate is like the frame and the *pond*, or the recessed center, is the canvas. Using a plate that may seem a bit large for the dish you are presenting is often times better than trying to squeeze things onto a smaller plate. The larger the canvas, the more room you will have to create your masterpiece. Most classic European restaurants will not place anything on the rim of the plate. This is not the case, however, with American restaurants. "Painting" plates, including the rims, has become very popular in restaurants in the US. This is achieved by way of a squeeze bottle with sauce.

Garnishing

Taste is the most important quality to consider when preparing or critiquing a meal, especially in a restaurant. The second most important factor is presentation. A dish should be plated in a manner that is appealing to the eye. Proper garnishing is a critical aspect of this eye appeal. Garnishes may be as simple as a sprig of fresh herb or a dusting of confectioner's sugar. They may also be complex, sometimes with the stature of a culinary skyscraper. The following are a few basic guidelines for and preparation of classic garnishes.

Garnishes for dishes that the guest will actually eat off of should be 100 percent edible, palatable, and compatible with the main item on the plate. Many times, a sample of the main item in the dish is used as a garnish to indicate what the dish is comprised of, e.g., a slice of cucumber to garnish a cucumber soup. Some herbs are chopped before being used as a garnish, while a *pluche*, or sprig, works better in some instances. Zest of citrus fruits can also be used as a garnish. However, most zest should first be blanched and shocked several times to remove the bitterness.

Garnishes that will be used in a buffet and will not be part of a diner's plate can be items that are edible, but not particularly palatable, such as tomato, orange, and lemon roses made from the skin of the fruit. The scale of garnishes for buffets is often much larger than those used for individual plates. Whole shellfish, watermelons, and heads of Savoy lettuce are just a few of the larger items used to garnish buffets. The same guideline of using an item that implies the dish is used for garnishing buffets. A watermelon burro can accentuate a Mexican buffet; a whole lobster adds panache to a seafood buffet; a carved head of Savoy can be used to hold dip for a crudité.

Roses are made by peeling the skin off a fruit or vegetable and twirling the whole skin into the shape of a flower. Tomatoes and citrus fruit work best for this. You must use a very sharp, thin bladed knife, such as a paring knife or slicer. The skin needs to be peeled in one piece. Start at the stem end by slicing a horizontal piece. This will become the base of the flower. Without separating the piece from the fruit, turn your knife ninety degrees and begin to peel the fruit. Continue around the fruit as many times as it takes to completely peel it, making sure that the skin is one piece. The thinner the peel, the better the flower will look. When you get to the bottom, sever the skin from the fruit. Place the part that you started with at the stem end on your work table and begin to twirl the remainder of the skin in a motion that will end up creating concentric rings that look like a rose.

Radish roses are carved rather than peeled. Carefully trim both ends of the radish. Holding the radish with the root end up, carefully carve the petals. The cuts should follow the curvature of the radish and overlap each other. Make sure not to slice all the way through the radish, thereby leaving the petals intact. You will need to soak the roses in cold water for a few hours or overnight in order for the flower to bloom.

You can make a green onion flower in a similar manner. Trim the root off the onion. Cut a piece three to four inches long. Make two to three longitudinal cuts on the green end. You will need to soak the flower in cold water in order for it to bloom, as you did for the radish rose.

You can make egg daisies from a hard-boiled egg by using an aspic cutter. Slice the egg in half; then take a thin slice of yolk from the center. This will be the center of the daisy. Using the teardrop aspic cutter, cut portions of the egg white and place them around the slice of yolk to look like petals. Use a long chive for the stem and place a leaf of basil on either side at the base.

You have probably seen palm tree carrots in a buffet or deli display. They are among the easiest of garnishes to make. You will need a large, straight carrot, a green bell pepper and a toothpick. Cut the large end of the carrot flat so that it can stand on this end. You may need to trim the other end so that it can support the green pepper top. Using a paring knife, make longitudinal slits in the skin of the carrot, from top to bottom, working your way around the carrot until it looks like the bark of a palm tree. Remove the top of the green pepper by making a series of cuts that would make it look like palm leaves. Attach the pepper to the top of the carrot by securing it with a toothpick. If your tree is unstable, you may steady it by placing a bit of peanut butter on the end. You can conceal the peanut butter by placing sprouts at the base to look like grass.

A very appropriate garnish for a cheese tray is a radish mouse. You will need a large radish with the root intact, a smaller radish, a couple of toothpicks, and some whole cloves. Slice a thin slice off one side of the large radish. The mouse will sit on this side. Using a toothpick, attach a trimmed small radish to the opposite end of the root. This will be the head. Trim a small piece out of each side of the top of the head for the ears. Carve two ears out of the piece that was removed from the bottom of the larger radish. Prop the pieces up in the slot to look like ears. Place a whole clove on the front of the head to look like a nose.

TABLE SETTINGS AND SERVICE

So far, the content of this book has largely covered **"back of the house"** issues, i.e., cooking and related kitchen issues. That's really only half of the formula for producing restaurant quality meals, especially when entertaining. The other half of the formula lies in the **"front of the house,"** which is the dining room. In order to provide a suitable venue for presenting the masterpieces that you produce in the kitchen, you will need to have some background information on table service and settings. There are many styles of table service, each with a specific table setting. Some of the most popular styles of service follow.

English Service
English table service is the style of service that most American households use for an informal family dinner. Food is placed in serving bowls and platters and passed to each member of the family so that they can create their own plate. The table setting that is most frequently used for these informal dinners is Modified Table D'Hôte (diagram follows).

American Service
American table service was invented by legendary restaurateur Howard Johnson in the mid-twentieth century. In this style of service, courses are served one at a time by removing the previous course's plate or bowl from one side of the diner while placing the new course from the other side. Beverages are always served and removed from the right. The table setting varies with the type of restaurant.

A La Carte Service
A la carte table service is the style that is most frequently used in fine dining restaurants. Courses are served one at a time and only the utensils needed for each particular course are placed on the table. All the utensils, plates, or bowls that are used for each course are removed from the table at the completion of that course and new utensils are laid in place for the next course.

Butler Service
Butler service is a modified version of English service that is used at the dining room tables of the wealthy. In this style of service, the food is served in large platters or bowls, similar to English service, but these platters and bowls are not

placed on the dining table. Waiters pass the items to each diner by presenting the food on the left side while the diner helps themselves to the items being served. Once again, beverages are always served and removed from the right. The table setting is almost always Table D'Hôte (see diagram).

French Service

In French table service, some or all of the dishes that are served are prepared at least in part tableside. These dishes often include the technique of *flambéing*, or flaming because of the presentation effect. The table setting is almost always a la carte.

Russian Banquet Service

Unfortunately, Russian Banquet Service is a vanishing style of service due to a lack of trained practitioners. It is the ultimate formal dining service. When carried out correctly it sometimes overshadows the food itself as far as being a contributor to the complete dining experience. The chef prepares large platters, often silver for each table of eight, including the portions of the item, garnish, and sauce. The waiters for each table line up at the dining room entrance with platters raised above their shoulders. The maître d' performs the duties of an orchestra conductor, as he or she signals the waiters to march into the dining room in cadence. Once each waiter arrives at their table; the maître d' signals for the service to commence. Each waiter then prepares the plates, one diner at a time in a synchronized fashion so that each waiter finishes at the same time. The waiters then wait for the maître d's signal to return to the kitchen. Every course is served in the same manner, with plates, bowls, and silverware being removed and set in place in a synchronized fashion.

a. *Service Plate:* This large plate, also called a charger, serves as an underplate for the plate holding the first course, which will be brought to the table. When the first course is cleared, the service plate remains until the plate holding the entrée is served, at which point the two plates are exchanged. The charger may serve as the underplate for several courses which precede the entrée.

b. *Butter plate:* The small butter plate is placed above the forks at the left of the place setting.

c. *Dinner fork:* The largest of the forks, also called the place fork, it is placed on the left of the plate. Other smaller forks for other courses are arranged to the left or right of the dinner fork, according to when they will be used.

d. *Fish fork:* If there is a fish course, this small fork is placed farthest to the left of the dinner fork because it is the first fork used.

e. *Salad fork:* If salad is served after the entrée, the small salad fork is placed to the right of the dinner fork, next to the plate. If the salad is to be served first, and fish second, then the forks would be arranged (left to right): salad fork, fish fork, dinner fork.

f. *Dinner knife:* The large dinner knife is placed to the right of the dinner plate.

g. *Fish knife:* The specially shaped fish knife goes to the right of the dinner knife.

h. *Salad knife:* If used, according to the above menu, it would be placed to the left of the dinner fork, next to the dinner plate. If the salad is to be served first, and fish second, then the knives would be arranged (left to right): dinner knife, fish knife, salad knife.

i. *Soup spoon or fruit spoon:* If soup or fruit is served as a first course, then the accompanying spoon goes to the right of the knives.

j. *Oyster fork:* If shellfish are to be served, the oyster fork is set to the right of the spoons. *Note: It is the **only** fork ever placed on the right of the plate.*

k. *Butter knife:* This small spreader is paced diagonally on top of the butter plate, handle on the right and blade down.

l. *Glasses:* These can number up to five and are placed so that the smaller ones are in front. The water goblet is placed directly above the knives. Just to the right goes a champagne flute; In front of these are placed a red and/or white wine glass and a sherry glass.

m. *Napkin:* The napkin is placed on top of the charger (if one is used) or in the space for the plate.

The Formal Table Setting

1. Sherry glass

2. White wine glass

3. Red wine glass

4. Water goblet

5. Oyster fork

6. Soup spoon

7. Dinner plate

8. Dinner fork

9. Salad/App fork

10. Dessert fork and spoon

11. Butter plate

Three Intimate Dinners to Dazzle Parents and Friends

Now that the table is set, it's time to create three menus for entertaining parents, family, or friends. The first two will be sit-down dinners that can be served a la carte. The third one will be a complete intimate dinner prepared and served tableside. Make sure that you set the table properly and that you have selected appropriate wine to go with each dish. Bread and butter should be at the table first and water glasses should be filled. Then, let the party begin.

Menu 1: A Cold Weather Menu

1st Course—Apple Smoked Prawns on Saffron Risotto Cake with Indian Style Chili Cream Sauce

2nd Course—Field Greens, Endive, and Radicchio Salad with Champagne Vinaigrette Dressing

Intermezzo—Grapefruit with Bitters and Sea Salt

Entrée—Grilled Filet Mignon with Shallot Marmalade

Dessert—New Orleans Bread Pudding with Chantilly Cream

Smoked Prawns on Saffron Risotto Cake with Indian Style Chili Cream Sauce (Serves 6)

There are three components to this dish, excluding garnishes: smoked prawns, sauce, and saffron risotto cakes. The word prawn is used to describe several members of the crustacean family, especially langoustines, spiny lobster, and Italian scampi. Very often, especially in the US, the word prawn is used to describe a very large shrimp, especially those in the U-12 category. Shrimp are sized according to the average number per pound. Accordingly, the lower the number in the description, the larger the shrimp. Typically, 16–20 and 21–25 are used in restaurants for a variety of dishes. Shrimp that are larger than 16–20 are named according to the maximum number per pound (e.g., U-12's contain *under* 12 shrimp per pound).

Risotto is an Italian rice dish that is prepared from the short grain *arborio* rice from the Po Valley. The preparation varies from that of long grain rice in that the ratio of liquid to rice is approximately three to one, as opposed to two to one for long grain rice and the technique is an open pot one, opposed to a covered pot technique. This method of preparation produces a more fluid and creamy product. The heated liquid is usually added in two to three portions, cooking the risotto with the lid off. Nearly constant stirring is a must, especially toward the end. Generally, the dish is finished with a sizable amount of butter and Parmesan cheese. Like long grain rice, you may use stock or water to prepare it and you may add seasoning vegetables, such as shallot, onion, or carrot.

Saffron Risotto Cakes

3–4 c. water	1 c. Arborio rice
½ t. saffron	1 t. salt
1 T. butter	½ t. white pepper

Heat the water to near boiling; add the saffron and hold the temperature. In a separate pot, melt the butter. Add the rice to the butter, stirring to coat. Add 1 cup water to the rice. Bring to a boil, stirring constantly. When the mixture becomes thick, add a second cup of water and repeat this process for a third cup. When the risotto becomes difficult to stir, test for doneness. The grains should be somewhat firm, not hard. If it needs more cooking, add a small amount of water and cook until done. Season with salt and white pepper. Spread the rice on a sheet pan or small cookie sheet in a layer that is 1–1 ½ inches thick. Refrigerate for 2–24 hours. Form the cakes by cutting with a 2-inch concentric cutter.

Spicy Indian Style Chili Cream Sauce

This sauce is a perfect example of how to convert a standard Sauce Tomàte to a sauce with a totally different flavor profile.

2 T. butter	t. cumin
1–2 jalapeño peppers, minced	2 t. coriander
1-inch piece ginger root, minced	½ c. cream
1 pint Sauce Tomàte (Pg. 134)	

Melt the butter in a small saucepot. Sweat the jalapeño and ginger root by cooking at medium heat for 2 minutes. Add the tomato sauce, cumin, and coriander, and simmer for 15 minutes. Stir in cream and cook another 2 minutes. Pass through a fine food mill and hold warm.

Smoking the Prawns and Plating the Dish

---

12 pieces of fried vermicelli (optional)
12 U-12 shrimp, peeled and deveined; tails intact
chopped cilantro

Fry the vermicelli in oil on top of the stove. Remove and reserve. Smoke the prawns over apple wood in a **Camerons Stovetop Smoker** for 5–8 minutes, or on an outdoor grill with apple wood. Reheat the rice cakes in a microwave oven and place them in the center of a ten-inch plate. Place 2 smoked prawns on top, standing them up with the tail upward and the bodies intertwined. Place three portions of sauce, about two ounces total, in a circle around the food. Garnish with chopped cilantro and two pieces of fried vermicelli, skewered into the rice cake.

Field Greens, Endive, and Radicchio Salad with Champagne Vinaigrette Dressing (Serves 4)

1 very long English cucumber, sliced thin lengthwise (a mandoline would be perfect here)	8 cherry tomatoes
	6 c. mixed field greens
2 heads Belgian endive	sprouts and four radish roses
1 head radicchio	1 recipe champagne vinaigrette dressing (recipe follows)
1 cluster Enoki mushrooms	

Make the radish roses (Pg. 154) and store in water in the refrigerator.

Champagne Vinaigrette Dressing

½ c. champagne vinegar	1 egg yolk
1 t. Dijon mustard	1 c. salad oil
1 T. shallot, minced	1 T. tarragon, chopped
1 t. honey	

Place the first 5 ingredients in a small bowl and slowly whisk in the oil to create an emulsion. Fold in the tarragon.

Plating

Make a well out of the cucumber strips by making a slit in one end, folding to make a circle and securing by inserting the other end into the slit. On each of four 10-inch plates, place four trimmed radicchio leaves at 12, 3, 6, and 9 o'clock. Place one leaf of endive inside each leaf of radicchio. Place a few enoki mushrooms inside the endive. Place one half cherry tomato on each leaf of Belgian endive. Place the cucumber well in the middle of the plate and fill with one cup of field greens that has been tossed with the dressing. Top with sprouts and a radish rose and sprinkle additional dressing around the outside of the cucumber well to decorate the plate and provide extra dressing.

Chilled Grapefruit with Bitters and Sea Salt Flakes **(Serves 4)**

1 C. sugar	Angostura Bitters
blue food coloring	Maldon sea salt flakes
12 sections of grapefruit, about 2 fruits	mint pluche for garnish

Color the sugar blue by adding blue food coloring and stirring to completely incorporate. Place on a saucer that is wider than the glass that the grapefruit will be served in. Take 4 glass pedestal cups or Marie Antoinette champagne glasses and invert them to rub the lip on a moist paper towel. Immediately immerse them in the colored sugar to coat the rim of the glass in the same way one would when prepping a Margarita glass. Place in the refrigerator to chill. Place 3 sections of grapefruit in each glass. Squirt a small amount of bitters on each. Top with a small amount of salt flakes. Garnish with mint.

Grilled Filet Mignon with Shallot Marmalade **(Serves 4)**

24 shallots, sliced	4 8–12 oz. beef filets, trimmed
1 qt. beef stock	kosher salt and coarse ground black pepper
1 qt. red wine	
2 T. sugar	oil to grill

Make the shallot marmalade a day ahead or the morning of your dinner party. Place the shallots, beef stock, wine, and sugar in a large sauce pot. Bring to a boil; then reduce the heat to simmer. Simmer several hours until almost all the liquid has evaporated and the shallots have formed a paste. Cool to room temperature.

Grill the steaks, either on an outdoor or stovetop grill. Rub with oil and season well with salt and pepper. Place on a hot grill for 3 minutes. Use the 10 o'clock; 2 o'clock grilling technique that was introduced in chapter 5 of this book to attain the proper grill marks. Grill 4–6 minutes per side, depending on how thick the steaks are, how hot the heat source, how close the steaks are to the flame, and the desired degree of doneness. **This requires practice.** If you are grilling the same type and size of steak on the same grill to the same degree of doneness over a period of time, you should be able to develop your own guidelines for how long to grill it on either side and which part of the grill to place it on. Initially, you can use a reliable meat thermometer, placed in the side of the steak to the middle to determine the degree of doneness. 125° for rare; 130° for medium rare; 135–140° for medium; 145–150° for medium-well; 155°+ for well done. Remove and serve on a bed of herbed faro (recipe follows) encircled with glazed julienne carrots (chapter 6) and topped with shallot marmalade.

Herbed Faro (Serves 4)

4	c. chicken stock	1	T. oregano, chopped
2	T. clarified butter	1	T. chives, chopped
1	c. leeks, minced	½	T. thyme, chopped
1	c. faro	2	T. whole butter
1	T. parsley, chopped		salt and white pepper to taste

Heat the stock to just below boiling in a small saucepot. In another pot, melt the clarified butter over medium-high heat and sweat the leeks by cooking until translucent and limp. Add the faro and toss to coat. Add one cup of the stock and cook until nearly dry. Add another cup of stock and repeat the process until all the stock has been added. Remove from the heat and fold in the whole butter and herbs. Season to taste with salt and white pepper.

New Orleans Bread Pudding with Chantilly Cream (Serves 4)

2	eggs	1 c. cream
¾	c. sugar	¼ c. raisins
1	t. vanilla	¼ c. roasted pecans, coarsely
1	t. nutmeg	chopped
1	t. cinnamon	3 c. stale French baguette bread, cut
3	T. butter, melted	into ½-inch cubes

Preheat the oven to 325° F. Beat the eggs in a stand mixer with the whip attachment, with a handheld mixer, or by hand until they are thick and frothy, about 3 minutes. Add the sugar, vanilla, nutmeg, cinnamon, and melted butter. Beat until well blended. Add the cream and beat 2 minutes. Fold in raisins and pecans. Place bread cubes in greased 4–6 ounce ramekins and pour the royale (the egg and cream mixture) over top. Cover until you see a thin layer on the sides. Soak for one hour. Bake in a 325° oven for 15 minutes. Increase oven temp to 425° and bake an additional 5 minutes. Serve warm or at room temperature, topped with Chantilly Cream (recipe follows) and placed on a small plate with a doily.

Chantilly Cream

2	c. heavy cream
1	t. vanilla
2	t. brandy or cognac
2	T. sugar

Place all ingredients in a chilled bowl and whip to soft peaks either by hand or with a handheld mixer.

Menu 2: A Summer Menu

1st Course—Cold Cantaloupe Soup with Pancetta

2nd Course—Champignons en Bouchée

Intermezzo—Macerated Strawberries with Balsamic Vinegar

Entrée—Poached Paupiette of Sole with Orange Beurre Blanc

Dessert—Fresh Fruit Cup with Zabaglione

Cold soups can be a pleasant surprise for your dinner guests and a welcome break in the food prep schedule for your next dinner party. Everyone is probably familiar with the classic French cold soup of potato and leek, called *vichyssoise* or the Spanish summer soup *gazpacho*. With a little creativity and some fresh produce, you can break out of the two-soup rut and impress your guests and family with an exciting new bill of fare.

There are two styles of cold soups from a preparation standpoint: those that require some cooking before being chilled, and those that are prepared in a food processor or blender without any cooking. Both are usually simple to prepare and may be stored in the refrigerator for 1–3 days prior to serving. This latter point can be a boon to the home chef who may wish to spend a bit more time with their friends on the day of their dinner party. Some cold soups, usually prepared from fruits, may be served as a dessert instead of a starter course.

Cold Cantaloupe Soup with Pancetta (Serves 4)

1 ripe cantaloupe, peeled, seeded, and cut into small chunks	2 T. Midori or other fruit liqueur
½ c. heavy cream	½ lb. pancetta, cooked and cut into ¼" dice
2 T. sugar	

Puree the cantaloupe in a blender. Add the cream, sugar, and liqueur. Process until well blended. Chill and serve in chilled bowls, garnished with the pancetta. Place the bowls on a plate with doily.

Champignons en Bouchée (Sautéed Mushrooms in Puff Pastry) (Serves 5)

6 puff pastry bouchés, available in frozen food section	½ c. heavy cream
1 lb. mushrooms, sliced	2 T. tarragon, chopped
2 T. butter, preferably clarified	salt and white pepper to taste
1 T. shallots, chopped	Sriracha chili sauce to paint the plates
½ c. dry white wine	

Bake the bouchés according to the directions on the box. Sauté the mushrooms in the butter at high heat until they are golden brown. Add the shallots and cook 2 minutes. Add the wine and reduce nearly to dryness. Add the heavy cream and 1 tablespoon of the tarragon. Reduce to one-half volume. Remove from the heat and season with salt and white pepper. Remove the tops to the bouchés and fill with mushrooms. Paint six 10-inch round white plates with Sriracha. Place the filled bouchés on top. Place the tops of the bouchés that were removed back on top to look like a propped lid. Garnish with fresh tarragon.

Macerated Strawberries with Balsamic Vinegar (Serves 6)

8 large strawberries	6 coupes or stemware, rims coated with blue colored sugar (Page 168) and chilled
2 T. sugar	
2 T. fine balsamic vinegar	6 sprigs of mint to garnish

Maceration is the softening and crushing of fruit under its own weight. It is sometimes used to make fine wine in a process called carbonic maceration. In the case of macerated strawberries, the softening agent is sugar, which is slightly acidic. Slice the strawberries in half and cover with the sugar. Place in a refrigerator for 4 hours. Place two halves in each coupe or stemware glass. Drizzle with high quality balsamic vinegar and garnish with mint.

Poached Paupiettes of Sole Served on a Bed of Sautéed Spinach with Orange Beurre Blanc Sauce
(Makes 8 Appetizer Servings or 4 Entrée Servings)

Paupiettes are thinly sliced pieces of meat or fish that are rolled into cups and filled with forcemeat. A forcemeat is an emulsion of fat and meat with flavorings that behaves like a single meat. Examples of forcemeats are pâtés, terrines, mousses, and mousselines. They are easily made in a food processor. The fat content is usually 25–50 percent. When making the emulsion, it is imperative that all the ingredients and equipment be as cold as possible so that the emulsion doesn't break when heated.

6	oz. scallops	2	oz. heavy cream
1	T. butter	½	t. white pepper
1	t. salt	6	oz. pasteurized lump crab meat

Chill the forcemeat ingredients along with the bowl and blade of the food processor. Place the scallops, butter, and salt in the bowl, fitted with the crushing blade. Turn on medium to chop and puree the ingredients. Slowly add the cream to form the emulsion. Season with pepper and fold in the crabmeat.

4	filets of sole or other fresh, flat fish	2	T. butter
		1	shallot, minced
1	c. white breadcrumbs tossed with	1	c. dry white wine
3	T. whole butter	1	c. fish stock

Preheat oven to 350° F. Split the sole filets in half along the lateral line. Form a cup and hold together with a toothpick. All fish filets have a skin side and a bone side to them. The bone side is usually more attractive than the skin side; so, when forming the paupiettes, make sure that the bone side is on the outside. Also, be sure to place the smaller end of the fillet on the inside of the cup and roll to cover and shape the cup. Transfer the forcemeat to a disposable pastry bag with no tip. Pipe the forcemeat into the cups. Top with white breadcrumbs. These can be made a couple of hours before meal time and stored in the refrigerator. Coat the bottom of a fry pan or rondeau with the butter. Spread the shallots over the bottom of the pan. Transfer the paupiettes to the pan. Add the wine and fish stock. Bring to a boil on top of the stove; then transfer to the 350°F oven and poach for 8–10 minutes. Meanwhile, sauté the spinach and make the beurre blanc sauce.

Orange Beurre Blanc Sauce (Makes 1 Cup)

Beurre Blanc Sauce is one of the most widely used and easiest to prepare sauces in French and American cuisines. It is an emulsion of an acid reduction and whole butter. It is generally prepared *a la minute*, literally at the last minute or to order. Standard Beurre Blanc Sauce starts with a reduction of wine and vinegar. Whole butter is then vigorously whisked into the sauce over very low heat. Sometimes the sauce is finished with cream to add flavor and stability. In the case of Orange Beurre Blanc Sauce, the reduction is orange juice. You can either reduce your own by starting with 1 cup of pulpless orange juice and reducing it to one-fourth its original volume in a saucepot over medium heat or you can just start with frozen concentrated orange juice. Both procedures produce essentially the same product.

---

3   T. frozen concentrated orange juice
1½ sticks whole butter, room temperature
salt and white pepper to taste

Chop the butter into small pieces. Place the orange juice in a small sauce pot and heat over medium heat to almost boiling. Reduce the heat to low and vigorously whisk in the whole butter in small portions. Season with salt and white pepper. Reserve in a warm (not hot) spot off the stove.

Sautéed Baby Spinach with Shallots (Serves 4)

1 lb. baby spinach, cleaned	1 small shallot, minced
1 T. clarified butter or olive oil	salt and white pepper to taste

Rinse the spinach and dry in a lettuce spinner. Heat the butter or oil to very hot in a large sauté pan or rondeau. Add the shallot, then the spinach. Season lightly with salt and white pepper, tossing the spinach in the hot pan until cooked. Do not overcook. Strain the excess liquid off in large strainer.

Divide the spinach evenly between 4 twelve-inch warm plates. Place it in the center of each plate to form a bed for the fish. Place two paupiettes on top of the spinach. Encircle the fish and spinach with two ounces of Orange Beurre Blanc Sauce.

Zabaglione with Fresh Fruit (Serves 4)

3–4 c. fresh fruit—melon, peaches, berries, kiwi—chopped
1   whole Egg + 2–3 Egg yolks
⅓   c. sugar
⅓   c. marsala wine
mint to garnish

Place the fruit in 4 coupes or other suitable stemware. In a double boiler, heat the egg, egg yolks, sugar, and wine while whisking vigorously until it forms a thin custard. Pour the zabaglione over the fruit, garnish with mint and serve, placing the coupes on a small plate with a doily.

Menu 3: Showing Off—A Complete Dinner Prepared Tableside

Whether it's an intimate candlelit dinner for two or a holiday gathering of friends, a dinner prepared tableside always adds a bit of panache to your dinner gathering. Tableside cooking requires preparation in order for the meal to proceed as planned. Choose a menu with an appropriate number of courses and plan each course so that you can keep up with the schedule and still manage to spend some quality time with your guests. Matching wine or spirits to each course will enhance the experience. If your dinner is for more than two, you may wish to enlist the aid of a friend who can help with drinks, clearing, bread and water service, etc. If you are not using a classic or published recipe, you should choose menu items that can be prepared quickly by using only a tabletop burner or cold items that require minimal preparation. All of the prep work—chopping, dicing, peeling, etc.—must be done before your guests arrive. These prepared items should be placed in small bowls that are dining room presentable. Some equipment that will help you maximize the experience are:

- A *guiridon*: a portable table with locking wheels. This is the platform on which most tableside dishes are prepared.
- A *rechaud*: a stand-alone burner used to prepare the majority of cooked tableside items. If you plan to flambé, this will need to be a gas burner.
- *Mise en place* bowls: the bowls or cups that contain the ingredients for each of the dishes that are prepared tableside.
- Bimetals, or copper cookware: Copper adds to the presentation of tableside cooking. Many desserts, in particular, are prepared in the shallow *Suzette* pan. You can also use a standard sauté pan, but it must be dining room worthy, i.e. impeccably clean.
- Wooden salad bowl for preparation of salads.

This sample dinner will be four courses. You should plan to eat each course with your guests in order to socialize and maximize the quality of the experience for yourself. In order to do so, you will need to do a considerable amount of advance prep. Each recipe will be broken down into this prep and the actual tableside prep.

Lobster Newburg over Toast Points (Serves 4)

Prepare Ahead

Make the Béchamel

1	T. butter, preferably clarified	1	c. half-and-half or heavy cream
2	T. onions, chopped	⅛	t. fresh ground nutmeg
1	T. flour		salt and white pepper to taste

In a small saucepot, melt the butter and sweat the onions by cooking until translucent. Add the flour and cook slowly for five minutes. Add the half-and-half, stirring constantly with a whisk. Bring to a boil, add the nutmeg, turn the heat down, and simmer 20–30 minutes. Season to taste with salt and white pepper and strain through chinois or China cap. Transfer to a *mise en place* cup.

Toast Points

4 thick slices bread
butter to brush on bread

Cut out four 3-inch diameter circles of bread with a round cookie cutter. Brush with butter and place under a broiler until brown, about 60 seconds. Cool and wrap in a cloth napkin; then place in a small basket or wooden bowl.

Have the above items prepped and place the items below in *mise en place* cups before the tableside presentation.

2	T. unsalted butter, preferably clarified	¼	c. dry Sherry
		1	T. shallot, finely chopped
2	c. lobster meat, claws and tail (available frozen), chopped	3	T. seafood stock
		¼	c. Parsley, chopped

Continued . . .

For the Tableside Preparation

Arrange the *mise en place* cups on the guiredon along with a gas burner, sauté pan, empty *mise en place* cup to contain the cooked lobster and four 10-inch plates. Heat a sauté pan over medium-high heat. Add 2 tablespoons butter and sauté the shallots 1 minute. Add the lobster meat and toss 1 minute. Add the sherry and cook to near dryness, about 2 minutes. Remove the lobster and place in the empty *mise en place* cup. Add the stock and Béchamel to the pan. Bring to a boil; reduce the heat and fold in the lobster. Place 1 toast point in the center of each plate. Top with lobster and sauce and garnish with chopped parsley.

Caesar Salad (Makes 4 servings)

Caesar Salad was created in Tijuana, Mexico, in 1924 by Italian chef Caesar Cardini. It was popularized in the fifties and sixties in the US and became a mainstay of tableside service in fine dining establishments. The original recipe calls for coddled egg in the dressing. This is a slow cook method where the egg is held in a container that is placed either in a poacher or a slow oven. Some restaurants will also coddle the egg by placing it in a bowl and pouring boiling water to cover it. In days gone by, the entire recipe, including dressing, was prepared tableside. Many restaurants have since gone to preparing the dressing ahead of time or removing the item from their menu altogether. This is due to the prevalence of *salmonella* bacteria in chicken and eggs. Preparing the dressing ahead of time allows the egg to become exposed to the acid found in the lemons and the salt in the anchovies, thereby decreasing the possibility of food borne illness. You can also use pasteurized eggs if you wish to prepare the dressing tableside.

Prepare Ahead

Make the croutons

---

4 slices country-style bread
2 T. olive oil or clarified butter
salt, pepper, garlic powder, and grated Parmesan cheese are optional

---

Slice the bread into ½–¾ inch cubes, excluding the crust. In a sauté pan at high heat, toss the cubes with the olive oil or clarified butter until they are golden brown. You may add salt, pepper, grated cheese, or garlic powder to impart extra flavor.

---

1 head Romaine lettuce

Chop the Romaine into bite-size pieces and thoroughly wash. Dry in a salad spinner. Wrap the lettuce in a clean white towel or napkin and place in a large *mise en place* bowl.

Prep the above items, and place the items below in *mise en place* bowls.

---

4 cloves garlic, three chopped finely, the other skewered on a fork	1½ t. fresh lemon juice*
4 filets of anchovy	2–3 egg yolks (pasteurized)
2 t. Dijon mustard	¾ c. Parmesan cheese, grated
	¾ c. extra virgin olive oil

Place these items, along with a large wooden salad bowl, four chilled salad or wooden salad bowls, a pair of salad tongs, and a pepper mill, on your portable table. The cheese bowl should also have a spoon to dispense. Season the wooden bowl by pressing the skewered garlic in a circular motion around the bowl. You may use a small amount of olive oil and salt to facilitate this process. When the bowl is seasoned, it will take on a darker appearance. Discard the garlic. Make the dressing. Smash the anchovies in the salad bowl, using the same fork that the garlic was skewered on. Add garlic and mustard and continue to stir and smash vigorously. You may also switch to a small whisk at this point. Add the lemon juice or squeeze it tableside through a lemon wrap. Whisk in the egg yolks. Whisk vigorously until well combined. Add **three-fourths** of the

Continued . . .

Parmesan cheese. While whisking, slowly add the olive oil to form a smooth dressing. Switch to the salad tongs. Add the Romaine and **half** the croutons and toss to coat the lettuce. Portion into salad bowls and garnish with the remaining croutons and additional Parmesan cheese. Top with fresh ground pepper for those who request it.

*For added presentation, place a half lemon in a lemon wrap with tie and squeeze tableside.

Steak Diane **(Makes 4 Servings)**

This is one of the most popular tableside entrees. It is traditionally made with quarter to half-inch thick *tournedos* or filet of beef. You can prepare it from any top quality steak that is boneless and thin enough to cook in a sauté pan.

Prepare Ahead

Make a Batch of Brown Sauce Espagnole

¼ c. clarified butter	1 T. parsley stems, chopped
½ c. onion, chopped	1 T. tomato paste or other tomato
¼ c. carrot, chopped	product
¼ c. celery, chopped	¼ c. flour
¼ c. turnip, chopped (optional)	32 oz. beef stock
¼ c. mushroom stems, chopped	1 bouquet garni of bay leaf and
1 t. garlic, chopped	thyme

In a 3-qt. saucepot, heat the butter to hot. Add the onion, carrot, and celery, and sauté until light brown. Add the turnip and mushroom stems and sauté until the onions and carrots are thoroughly caramelized and dark brown. Add the garlic and parsley stems and cook to aroma, about 30 seconds. Add the tomato product and cook an additional 30 seconds. Add the flour and make a brown roux the consistency of wet sand at low tide. You should lower the heat to make the roux, and cook for at least 10 minutes. Add the beef stock and bring to a boil. Add the bouquet garni, lower the heat, and simmer for at least 2 hours. During this time, you will need to skim the material from the top every 20–30 minutes. Strain through fine China cap or chinois. Season with salt and white pepper.

Slice eight ½-inch thick pieces of filet or have the butcher do that. Two tournedos each is the usual portion size. However, you may serve three. Place on a large plate and chill. Slice 20 ounces of mushrooms and place in a glass or porcelain bowl.

Assemble all other ingredients below, and place in *mise en place* bowls.

4	T. clarified butter	1	c. Brown Sauce Espagnole
2	T. shallot, chopped	½	c. heavy cream
2	t. Dijon mustard		salt to taste
¼	c. unflavored brandy		chopped parsley for garnish

Place all ingredients on movable table along with a *rechaud*, pepper mill, a pair of tongs, wooden spoon, a clean platter to hold the reserved cooked steaks, four 12-inch dinner plates, and copper sauté pan. Season the steaks with salt and pepper. Heat the pan over the *rechaud* and add a small amount of clarified butter. Sauté the steaks 2–4 at a time, to rare, about 90 seconds on a side. Remove and place on a plate. Add the mushrooms and thoroughly sauté. Add the shallot and cook one minute. Add the mustard and stir to combine. Remove completely from the flame and add the brandy. *Never add brandy or any other liquor to a pan that is on a burner!* Return to the burner and tilt the pan slightly to flambé. When the flames subside, add the Brown Sauce and bring to a boil. Whisk in the cream and bring to a boil. Return the steaks to the pan and cook to desired degree of doneness. Serve immediately, garnishing with chopped parsley.

Bananas Foster over Vanilla Ice Cream (Serves 4)

There are several versions, not only of this recipe, but also of the story of its origin. The story we will offer is that it originated at Brennan's Restaurant in the *Veaux Carré* section of New Orleans. The original recipe calls for using Meyers Rum and Crème de Banane. We will use unflavored brandy. It is very easy to make and goes well over top of vanilla ice cream.

Prepare Ahead

Make the vanilla ice cream the day before, or purchase ½ gallon of high quality vanilla ice cream

Vanilla Ice Cream (Yields 1 Quart)

Note: This recipe requires the use of an ice cream machine

2   c. heavy or whipping cream
¾   c. sugar
2   t. vanilla extract
⅔   c. half-and-half

Pour the cream into a mixing bowl. Whisk in the sugar, a little at a time; then continue whisking until completely blended, about 1 minute more. Pour in the vanilla and half-and half and whisk to blend. Follow the instructions on your ice cream maker to process into ice

cream. When ice cream is done, transfer to a plastic container with tight-fitting lid and freeze at least 2 hours.

Place four ice cream bowls in the freezer. Just before serving, place one scoop of ice cream in each bowl.

Assemble the ingredients below in *mise en place* bowls.

2   T. butter
½   c. brown sugar
4   bananas, cut into quarters*
1   t. cinnamon
¼   c. unflavored brandy

Place all ingredients on the movable cart along with a wooden spoon, a sauté pan, the chilled bowls with ice cream, and the *rechaud*. Heat the pan over the *rechaud* and add the butter and brown sugar. Cook until it forms a syrup. Add the bananas and cinnamon and cook until soft. **Remove from the burner and add the brandy.** *Again, never add brandy or any other liquor to a pan that is on a burner!* Return to the burner and flambé. When the flames subside, boil an additional minute. Serve in small bowls or over ice cream.

*Slice the bananas in half lengthwise first; then slice into quarters but cutting them in half across the smaller side.

CHAPTER TEN

A Complete Hors D'oeuvres Menu for a Cocktail Party

You are entering the final phase of your transition from a Rookie Cook to a self-reliant cook. You have mastered kitchen safety and sanitation, cook's ingredients, classic techniques, sauces, basic cooking, meal planning, and entertaining for a small sit down dinner. It's time to celebrate by throwing a party. You're going to pull from all that you have learned so far to make your party an unforgettable experience for your friends and family.

The menu we will cover will be a cocktail party menu of finger food hors d'oeuvres. The style of service will be part buffet and part butler style (passed by a waiter). The service should allow for guests to sample food while holding a drink. You should allow at least three months for planning your event. Depending on the size of the party, you may need to rent some equipment, tables, and chairs; and you may need to hire a temporary wait staff. The former can be done through your local party rental store. The latter can be set up through most caterers. You may wish to rent a speed rack to store the sheet pans on which your hors d'oeuvres are constructed.

Hors d'oeuvres are French appetizers. They may be plated and served as the first course in a multi-course meal or assembled in bite-size portions that are passed butler-style at a party. The only hard and fast rule of preparing hors d'oeuvres is that the portion should be small and the flavor should be exciting.

In American restaurants, plated hors d'oeuvres have evolved into mini-meals. The seven-inch appetizer plate has become nearly extinct as chefs opt for larger canvases to display their works of art. Just as in the world of main courses, contemporary appetizer plating tends to be center plate and tall. Garnishes often overwhelm the main item. Hors d'oeuvres that are passed or served buffet style are best described as finger food. The platters they are served from are sometimes elaborately garnished, as opposed to the individual garnishing found in plated appetizers.

Canapés are open-faced Swedish sandwiches. They are a type of hors d'oeuvres. They are most frequently passed butler-style at parties and are therefore generally bite-size. There are four components to a canapé: a base, a body, a spread, and a garnish. Many times, two or more of these components may be combined into one.

There are three phases to planning and executing an hors d'oeuvres menu. The first is the **conceptual phase**. This is where the imagination conjures up a menu. Menus should have balance between hot and cold hors d'oeuvres. They should also be reflective of the season. Cold soups, for instance, served in disposable soufflé or pedestal cups are most appropriate for the summer. Some hors d'oeuvres should be passed and others served in a buffet; especially hot hors d'oeuvres that are served from a chafing dish. In arranging an hors d'ouevres menu, it is important to have variety of taste, shape, composition, texture, and color. Remember that most people in a non-sit down format will have a drink in hand. Therefore canapés and hors d'ouevres should be just a bite and not sloppy. You should plan on having at least one or two canapés that are piped out of a pastry bag so that the production end proceeds expeditiously.

The second phase of planning and executing an hors d'oeuvres menu is the **production phase.** Once the prototype for each individual hors d'oeuvres is set, the production phase is a bit like manufacturing. That being the case, all components of a canapé—bases, spreads, bodies, and garnishes—must be prepped and ready for assembly prior to actually making them. In determining the amounts to prepare, you should allow for 6 canapes or small pieces of hot or cold hors d'ouevres for each guest during the first hour of the party and one each for every hour after that.

Bases are sometimes called supports. They are most frequently some type of cocktail bread, usually toasted. Sometimes a cracker is used for the same purpose. Other supports may be vegetables or fruits. When preparing a series of canapés, varying the shape of the supports is important. Three basic shapes for cocktail bread supports are circles, squares, and triangles. Using specific cookie or aspic cutters may produce other shapes. The crust should always be removed from cocktail bread before constructing a canapé. The supports can be prepared well in advance—crust removed, cut into various shapes, toasted—and stored in Ziploc bags.

Spreads or sauces for canapés are mostly cold dressings, such as mayonnaise, mustard, hot sauces, or a combination thereof. Many times they are applied directly to the support before placing the body on top. Sometimes they are placed on top of the canapé and may double as a garnish. Sometimes they are incorporated into the body, as in a meat or fish salad. The list of possible spreads is nearly unending. Spreads mainly influence the taste of the product.

The **body** is the main component of the canapé. It may be meat, fish, vegetables, or cheese. It could also be pâté, mousse, or pesto. The qualities that are impacted most by the body are taste, texture, and composition.

Garnishes mostly influence the color of the product. However, they could impact the taste and perhaps the texture. Garnishes should complement and even replicate the body of the canapé and should always be a supporting character.

Once all the components of the canapés are prepped, they are assembled in production line fashion, usually on sheet pans. Bases are laid out on the sheet pans and the remainder of the canapé is constructed on them. They are then stored in a refrigerator or on a speed rack.

The final phase of preparing and serving an hors d'oeuvres menu for a cocktail party is the **presentation phase.** This where the stored canapés and hors d'oeuvres are transferred to serving platters or chafing dishes. Fried hors d'oeuvres are best stored under a heat lamp. Cold hors d'oeuvres and canapés can be served butler style off platters that are garnished with some of the items covered in Chapter 12 of this book. The following menu is a mixture of hot and cold hors d'oeuvres and canapés. In constructing a menu, choose 3–5 hot and 3–5 cold items based on the number of people being served and time of year.

Mini Maryland Crab Cakes with Sauce Remoulade
(Makes 30–40 Mini Crab Cakes)

1	lb. lump or claw crabmeat		T. parsley, chopped
2	egg yolks + two whole eggs	2	t. Dijon mustard
2	t. Worcestershire sauce		t. Old Bay Seasoning
½	t. Tabasco	½	c. cracker crumbs or panko bread
1	T. shallot, chopped		crumbs

Preheat oven to 350° F. Spread the crabmeat on a cookie sheet and pick through to remove any shells. In a small bowl, thoroughly blend together the egg yolks, eggs, Worcestershire, Tabasco, shallot, parsley, mustard, and Old Bay. In a large bowl, gently toss the crabmeat with the seasoning mixture. Fold in the cracker crumbs. Gently form into very small cakes. You may use a one-ounce scoop or disher for portion control. Place on a cookie sheet and refrigerate at least one hour. Place in 350°F oven for 10–12 minutes, until golden brown. Serve out of a chafing dish with Sauce Remoulade.

Sauce Remoulade

1	c. mayonnaise	1	T. capers
1	T. shallot, chopped	1	boiled egg, chopped
½	t. Tabasco	1	T. Dijon mustard
1	t. Worcestershire Sauce	1	T. fresh lemon juice

Place all ingredients in a small bowl and mix well.

Curried Chicken Mousse on Brown Bread (Makes 30–40 Canapes)

1 lb. chicken breast, boneless and skinless	⅓ c. heavy cream
2 t. kosher salt	36 slices brown cocktail bread, cut into rounds and toasted
1 t. Madras Curry Powder	dried currants for garnish
¼ t. red pepper	

Poach the chicken breasts in salted water or chicken stock until cooked thoroughly. Refrigerate until cold. Refrigerate a food processor bowl with macerating blade. Place the chicken and spices in the food processor and process until fully pureed. With food processor running, slowly add chilled cream to form a smooth mousse. Place the mousse in a pastry bag with a star tip. Top each support with mousse; garnish with a single currant.

Toasted Pecan Pesto on English Cucumber with Pimento (Makes 16 canapes)

16 slices English cucumber	3 T. parmesan cheese
½ c. pecans, toasted	1–2 T. olive oil
2 T. basil, chopped	dash of Tabasco
1 t. garlic, chopped	pimento slices for garnish

Place the toasted pecans, basil, garlic, and cheese in a small food processor, equipped with the maceration blade. Process on high for 30 seconds. Slowly add the oil to form a pesto. Season with Tabasco. Using a small disher or melon scoop, place a small mound of pesto on each cucumber slice. Garnish with two slices of pimento, forming an "X."

Saga Bleu Cheese with Granny Smith Apple on Water Cracker
(Makes 16 Canapes)

16 small slices Granny Smith apple
¼ lb. Saga bleu cheese
lemon wasabi sauce (Available in supermarkets)
16 English water crackers

Prepare 16 small slices of Granny Smith apple and coat with lemon. Cut the cheese into 16 small portions. Spread the lemon wasabi on each cracker. Top with cheese and garnish with apple.

Liverwurst Mousse on Brown Bread with Cornichon
(Makes 16 Canapes)

¼   lb. liverwurst, preferably smoked
2–3 T. heavy cream
16   triangular slices cocktail bread, toasted
salt and white pepper to taste
16   small slivers cornichons

Preheat oven to 350° F. Chill the components of a small food processor, along with the liverwurst and cream. Remove the crust from the bread, cut in half diagonally to produce small triangles, and toast lightly on a sheet pan in a 350°F oven. Place the liverwurst, salt, and pepper in the food processor, equipped with the maceration blade. Turn on and slowly add the cream to form a mousse. Place the mousse in a pastry bag, fitted with the star tip. Pipe the mousse onto each support and garnish with gherkin sliver.

Creamy Butternut Squash Soup in Demitasse
(Makes 4 full portions or a full tray of demitasse portions)

1 medium butternut squash,	¼ t. white pepper, freshly ground
1 T. butter	½ c. heavy Cream, plus more for
2 t. onions, chopped	garnish
2 c. chicken stock	chiffonade of sage for garnish
½ t. kosher salt	

Preheat oven to 350° F. Cut the butternut squash in half and place on a roasting pan, cut side down. Pour about ¼ inch of water into the pan and place in the oven. Roast for about 1½ hours or until the squash is soft to the touch. Sweat the onions in the butter. Scrape the squash out of its skin with a spoon and add to the onions along with the chicken stock. Simmer until all the mixture is tender enough to puree easily. Puree using a standing or immersion blender. If necessary, add more stock or water to adjust consistency, and strain through a sieve. Return to the pot to reheat. Whisk in ½ cup heavy cream, making sure not to boil or the soup will separate. Adjust the seasonings if necessary. The soup may be held in a large teapot or other covered pitcher. To serve, pour into demitasse and garnish with a swirl of cream or a dollop of unsweetened whipped cream and sage leaves

Crab Mornay in Mini Tart Shells

This is a quick and easy hors d'oeuvre that is elegant in composition and presentation. Make the Béchamel a day ahead, and the dish goes together in a matter of minutes.

36 mini tart shells, premade	¼ c. Parmesan cheese, grated
1 lb. crabmeat	1–2 T. clarified butter
1 pint thick Béchamel Sauce	1 T. shallot, chopped
(recipe follows)	½ c. dry white wine
½ c. swiss cheese, shredded	

Béchamel Sauce

4 T. butter, preferably clarified	1 bay leaf
⅓ C. onions, chopped	½ t. fresh ground nutmeg
4 T. flour	salt and white pepper to taste
1 qt. half-and-half or heavy cream	

In a small saucepot, melt the butter and sweat the onions by cooking until translucent. Add the flour and cook slowly for five minutes. Add the half-and-half, stirring constantly with a whisk. Bring to a boil, add the bay leaf and nutmeg, turn the heat down, and simmer 20–30 minutes. Season to taste with salt and white pepper and strain through chinois or China cap.

Make the Béchamel a day ahead and refrigerate. Pick through the crabmeat to remove any shell. Heat the Béchamel in a small saucepot to simmering. Add the cheeses and stir to thoroughly combine. This is Sauce Mornay. Remove from heat and set aside. In a medium sauté pan, heat the butter over medium-high heat. Add the shallot and cook 30 seconds. Add the crab and stir 30 seconds. Add the wine and reduce to almost dryness. Add the Mornay Sauce and stir to heat. Remove from the heat and fill each of the tart shells.

Whipped Mascarpone and Gorgonzola on Plantain Chip with Mango (Makes 32 Canapes)

½ c. onion, minced	4 oz. mascarpone cheese
2 anchovy filets	½ T. dry mustard
1 T. capers	½ t. Tabasco
½ c. scallion, minced	32 plantain or lentil chips
8 oz. Gorgonzola cheese	32 small slivers of mango

Place the onion, anchovy, capers, and scallion in a mini-chop food processor and puree. Transfer to a larger food processor and add the cheeses, mustard, and Tabasco. Puree until smooth. Transfer to a pastry bag with a star tip. Pipe onto chips and garnish with mango.

Mini Egg Rolls with Duck Sauce

1½ t. vegetable oil	2 t. sesame oil
½ t. ginger, minced	1½ t. kosher salt
1 T. scallion, white, thinly sliced	¼ t. ground white pepper
2 T. scallion, green, julienned	6 oz. chicken breast, poached and
8 oz. Napa cabbage	finely shredded or chopped
4 oz. bean sprouts	50 wonton wrappers
2 t. soy sauce, dark	egg wash made with 1 egg and 2 t.
2 t. rice wine	water

Heat oil in wok; add ginger and scallions. Stir-fry until aromatic.

Add cabbage, bean sprouts, and scallion greens; stir-fry until all vegetables are cooked. Add soy sauce, rice wine, sesame oil, sugar, salt, and pepper. Mix together, drain excess liquid. Remove from heat, cool, and add chicken. Preheat frying oil to 350° F in a deep fryer. Place ½ teaspoon of filling on each wonton wrapper; brush edges of sheet with egg wash. Fold in about ¼ inch on left and right side of wrapper. Roll the wrapper away from you and seal. Set aside. Just before serving, deep fry at 350°f until golden brown; drain on paper towels.

Spanish Tuna Tapenade in Peppadew with Marcona Almond (Makes 12)

8 oz. Spanish tuna	12 peppadew peppers
¼ c. olive oil	12 Marcona almonds

Place the tuna in a minichop and process until it forms a paste. Slowly drizzle the olive oil in with the motor running to form the tapenade. Place in a pastry bag and pipe into the peppers. Garnish with almond.

Mini Open Face Burgers with Rooster Sauce

6–8 slices bread—white, wheat, or rye	1 T. Worcestershire sauce
	½ t. Tabasco
1 lb. ground buffalo or lean ground sirloin	32 dill pickle slices
	Rooster Sauce (Sriracha) to garnish

Preheat oven to 350° F. With a 1¼-inch round cutter, cut out 32–36 pieces of bread. Place on a sheet pan and toast in the oven for 5–8 minutes, until slightly toasted. Cool and store in a Ziploc bag. Combine the meat, Worcestershire, and Tabasco in a bowl. Form 1/2 oz. hamburgers with a disher and place on a greased sheet pan. Cover with another greased sheet pan to prevent the burgers from becoming meat balls. Bake in a 350°F oven for 10–15 minutes, until cooked. Drain off excess fat. Assemble the burgers by placing one dill slice on each toast round, topping with a mini burger and garnishing with Rooster Sauce. Skewer each with a cocktail toothpick.

Chorizo, Quince Paste, and Manchego Cheese on Toast (Makes 24 Canapes)

24	slices toasted cocktail bread, cut into 1" rounds
6	oz. smoked or dried chorizo sausage
¼	lb. Manchego cheese
3–4	oz. quince paste, cut into 24 small slices

Cut and toast the cocktail bread and store in a Ziploc bag. Cut the chorizo into ½-inch slices. Grate the cheese on the teardrop side of a box grater. Place one slice of quince paste on each toast round, top with chorizo and cheese, and melt in a broiler for 30–60 seconds. Serve warm.

Limoncello Grilled Shrimp (Makes 30–40 Shrimp)

2 lb. 16–20 Shrimp, peeled and deveined	¼ c. limoncello
15–20 small bamboo skewers, soaked in water for an hour	1 c. fresh chopped marjoram
	¼ c. extra-virgin olive oil
grated zest and juice of 2 lemons	1 t. red pepper flakes
	1 t. salt

Skewer two shrimp on each skewer by placing them with tails opposite each other and bodies entwined. Place them in a Ziploc bag with the remainder of the ingredients. Marinate in the refrigerator for 2–3 hours, shaking the bag occasionally. Start the fire 30 minutes prior to grilling. Grill the shrimp for 3 minutes, turn, and grill an additional 1½ minutes. Serve warm or at room temperature. Long, thick rosemary branches may also be used as skewers.

Grilled Lamb Pimentón (Makes 24 to 36 Skewers)

1 lb. Boneless lamb, cut into ½-inch cubes	½ T. kosher salt
½ c. Extra virgin olive oil	1 T. hot Hungarian paprika
3 T. garlic, minced	2 T. Pimentón (smoked paprika)
	¼ c. parsley, chopped

Place the lamb in a plastic bag along with ½ cup olive oil, the garlic, paprika, pimentón, salt, and parsley. Marinate at least 30 minutes, and up to 2 hours. Skewer the lamb and grill until medium or medium-rare.

Peanut Butter and Bacon on Ritz (Makes 24 Canapes)

¼ lb. cooked bacon
½ c. peanut butter
24 Ritz crackers

Chop the bacon into bits. Spread peanut butter on each cracker. Top with bacon. Place under a broiler for 1 minute.

Smoked Mussels on Brown Bread with English Mustard (Makes 24)

24 slices brown bread, cut into circles and toasted
¼ c. coleman's English Mustard
24 smoked mussels
chives, chopped, for garnish

Spread the mustard on the toasted support and top with a single mussel. Garnish with chives.

Smoked Salmon on Rye Toast with Dijonnaise Sauce (Makes 24)

24 slices of rye cocktail bread, crust removed and toasted
½ c. mayonnaise
3 T. dijon mustard
24 strips of smoked salmon, 1½ inch by 3 inch
olive oil to brush
capers to garnish

Make the Dijonnaise sauce by mixing the mayonnaise and mustard. Spread a small amount on each toasted support. Place a slice of salmon on each, folding the long end over to form a square. Brush lightly with olive oil and garnish with 2–3 capers.

Salmon Mousse in Cherry Tomato Timbale with Cornichon **(Makes 36 canapes)**

½ lb. cured salmon	36 cherry tomatoes
½ t. lemon juice	cornichon slices for garnish
⅓ C. heavy cream	

Refrigerate a food processor bowl with macerating blade. Place the salmon in the food processor and process until fully pureed. Add lemon juice. With food processor running, slowly add chilled cream to form a smooth mousse. Wash the tomatoes and remove the stem end. Reserve the tops. Remove the inside of the tomato with a melon scoop. Remove a small slice off the bottom of each tomato so that they sit flat. Place the mousse in a pastry bag with a star tip. Fill each tomato with mousse; garnish each tomato with slice of cornichon.

Cold Cucumber Soup in Demitasse **(Makes 20–30 Servings)**

4 large cucumbers, peeled, seeded, and sliced	½ c. unflavored yogurt
large shallot, chopped	½ c. sour cream
juice and zest of one large lemon	1 c. heavy cream or buttermilk
1 pint chicken stock, chilled	½ t. thyme
⅔ c. mayonnaise	salt and white pepper to taste
	lemon zest for garnish

Puree cucumbers and shallot with lemon juice in a food processor or blender, thinning with chicken stock, as needed. Place the contents in a large bowl and whisk in the mayonnaise, yogurt, and sour cream. Blend in the cream or buttermilk and season with thyme, salt, and white pepper. Chill the soup in a refrigerator for 2–72 hours. Reseason with salt and white pepper if necessary, just prior to serving. Serve in demitasse cups or small disposable soufflé cups, garnishing with lemon zest.

DO NOT TURN THIS PAGE BEFORE READING THE PASSAGE BELOW!!!

You have completed your maiden voyage into the wonderful world of culinary art. You have worked your way up the cooking pyramid from sanitation and kitchen safety to stocking your pantry, to getting into the kitchen and eventually dazzling your family and friends with your newly found skills. Now that you have confidence, knowledge, and cooking skills, many other journeys await. The extent of those journeys is only limited by your imagination. And now, you have earned the right to turn this page because you are a . . .

APPENDIX ONE

Herbs and Spices

B eyond the basic ingredients and the technique used to prepare a dish, herbs and spices are what accentuates each preparation and makes it unique. The following is a list of common herbs and spices used for cooking.

Adobe Seasoning: also called adobo or dobe. The ultimate seasoning for Latin cuisine. Used in Cuban, Dominican, Puerto Rican, and other Latin cuisines. Can be used as a rub for meat, fish, or veggies. Can also be sprinkled on chips or onion rings or used to liven up the flavor of dips.

Allspice: pea-sized berry of the evergreen pimiento tree. It is native to Jamaica and South America and is one of the key ingredients in jerk seasoning as well as pies and tarts.

Amchoor: an East Indian seasoning made by pulverizing dried green mango to a fine powder. Used to tenderize and flavor meats, vegetables, and curries.

Anise: ancient spice, probably of Mediterranean origin. Both leaves and seeds have a characteristic licorice flavor. Used to infuse Ouzo, Arrack, Pastis, and Anisette. Also used in confections and as a digestif in Indian cuisine.

Annatto: also called achiote. Comes from the achiote seed and is used mainly as a coloring agent, most notably in margarine and Mexican rice.

Arrowroot: derived from the dried root of the plant of the same name. Arrowroot is one of the most ideal thickening agents in all of cooking. It has twice the thickening capacity of wheat flour, is virtually tasteless, and becomes clear when cooked. Like cornstarch, it should be slurried in cold water before using.

Asafetida: a flavoring obtained from a plant in the fennel family. Used in East Indian cooking. It has a fetid, garlicky smell and should be used in small quantities.

Basil: a prominent member of the mint family. The essential ingredient in Italian pesto. Used for a variety of Italian dishes, from sauces to salads. Its flavor has been described as a cross between licorice and cloves.

Bouquet Garni: a group of herbs tied together to season stocks, soups, and stews. Usually contained in cheesecloth for easy removal. Classic combination is parsley, thyme, and bay leaf, although there are many other variations.

Caraway Seed: a member of the parsley family. It has a nutty, slightly anise flavor and is used in German, Austrian, and Hungarian cuisine. It is the seed that is found on the outside of Jewish rye bread.

Cardamom: a member of the ginger family. Tiny seeds encapsulated in pods, it's used to make teas and to season curries and other East Indian dishes.

Carob: a substitute for chocolate. Comes from the pods of the carob plant that are dried, roasted, and ground into a powder. It is used in candies and other confections and is also a laxative.

Celery Seed: seed of the wild celery plant called lovage. Indigenous to India, it has a pronounced flavor and is used in pickling and to flavor soups, salads, and other dishes. Use sparingly.

Chervil: a relatively rare member of the parsley family. It has a delicate licorice flavor and is one of the herbs found in *fines herbes*. Also called cicily and sweet cicily.

Chili Guajillo: a long, narrow, dried chile with a tough, shiny skin. Also called *travieso* ("mischievous") *chile* because of its reputation as a surprisingly hot spice. Used for sauces and other dishes.

Chinese Five Spice: combination of five Chinese spices in equal amounts: cinnamon, cloves, star anise, fennel seed, and Szechuan peppercorns. Used in a wide variety of Asian dishes, especially stir-fries.

Chives: a member of the alium family, which includes onions and leeks. Very slender, long green stems that are usually snipped and used to flavor salads, sauces, and sour cream that is used as a baked potato topping.

Cilantro: the leaves of the coriander plant, a member of the parsley family. It is also called Chinese parsley. It is used extensively in Mexican and East Indian cuisine and its flavor is sometimes described as "soapy."

Cinnamon: the inner bark of a tropical evergreen tree. It is used extensively in baking and to season teas and hot drinks. In stick form, it is used for pickling and to prepare Indian Basmati rice.

Clove: a very distinctive, strong spice that is the bud of an oriental evergreen tree. Sold whole or ground, they are used sparingly in baking and in East Indian cuisine, as well as to spice ham.

Coriander: the seeds of the plant of the same name. Sold whole or ground, it is one of the chief ingredients in Indian curry powder. Also used for pickling, the leaves are called cilantro.

Cumin: also called comino. Ancient spice that is the dried seeds of a member of the parsley family. Used extensively in Mexican, East Indian, and Middle Eastern cuisine. It is sold in seed and ground form and is one of the key seasonings in chili.

Curry Leaf: leaf from a small plant native to southern Asia. It looks like a small lemon leaf and has a pronounced curry flavor.

Dill: ancient herb that is used to season salads and other dishes. Must be used right away to ensure potency. Also used to prepare pickles. The dry form is much weaker in flavor.

Epazote: used in Mexican cooking to flavor beans. It renders a pungent flavor and is a carminative (reduces gas). Also called Mexican tea (for which it is used), and wormseed.

Fennel: a member of the celery family, all parts of the plant are used in cooking. The stem and fronds are used fresh for salads and in cooking lamb and pork. The dried seeds are used whole to season meat and vegetable dishes. It has a licorice flavor.

Fenugreek: ancient spice of Asia and Southern Europe. Pleasantly bitter, slightly sweet seeds are used to make teas, curry powder, and other spice blends.

Flaxseed: primarily used to make linseed oil, a base for varnishes, paints, and ink. Seeds are high in omega-3 fatty acids and have therefore become a popular food supplement, especially for vegetarians. When ground and combined with water, it forms a gelatinous blend approximately the consistency of egg whites and therefore is used as an egg replacer in recipes.

Galangal: a root similar in taste to ginger. Used mainly in Thai cooking, it has a zestier flavor than ginger root. Sometimes called Laos, Thai, or Siamese ginger. Great for Thai stir-fry.

Garlic: a member of the alium family. It is one of the most widely used ingredients in cooking. It is found in nearly every cuisine from Asian to French to Italian to Regional American. It has a more pronounced flavor than its close relative the onion, and is therefore used in smaller quantities.

Ginger: used both fresh as ginger root and dried and ground. It is used in many Asian cuisines and has a distinctive citrus sweet flavor. Also used in teas and for medicinal purposes.

Green Peppercorns: underripe berry of the same plant that yields both black and white peppercorns. Usually preserved in brine, it has a fresher flavor than either white or black peppercorns. With a flavor much like a spicy juniper berry, it is used in sauces and in pâtés.

Herbes de Provence: a blend of herbs that is supposed to reflect those that are used most frequently in southern France. Usually contains basil, fennel, lavender, marjoram, rosemary, sage, summer savory, and thyme.

Horseradish: one of the five bitter herbs of the Jewish Passover. Used fresh, it is first grated and is a powerful lachrymator. Prepared versions are used as spicy hot, aromatic condiments for seafood and vegetables and combined with ketchup to make cocktail sauce.

Jasmine Flower: A fragrant, aromatic flower of the genus and species *Jasminum officinale*. Used to make herbal teas. Caffeine content accounts for the mood and energy boost associated with consumption. Other non-culinary applications include herbal pillows, soaps, and potpourri.

Jerk Seasoning: a Jamaican dry rub for grilled meats and seafood. Ingredients vary, but a true jerk seasoning contains chilies, allspice, and assorted herbs such as thyme, and spices like cinnamon and cloves.

Juniper Berry: astringent blue-black berry native to Europe and America. It has a pronounced pine flavor and is used for marinades and to infuse gin.

Lavender: a relative of mint, it has pale green leaves and purple flowers, both of which are used to flavor salads and make tea.

Mace: the bright red membrane that covers the nutmeg seed. More pungent than nutmeg, mace is used to season both savory and sweet dishes, like pumpkin pie.

Marjoram: of Greek origin, this herb has a flavor that is very similar to oregano—a fact that makes it a common substitute for that herb.

Masalas: a masala is a mixture of spices used to season Indian and Pakistani dishes. The most popular masala is **garam masala**, which is comprised of 4–6 spices depending on which region it comes from. Other masalas include **Punjabi masala, tandoori masala, tiki masala, sambaar masala, and curry powder.**

Mint: there are many varieties of this sweet aromatic herb. The most common types are spearmint and peppermint. It is used in drinks and tea, desserts, and sauces.

Mojo Seasoning: a mojo is a juice-based sauce that is usually combined with vegetables like garlic and onion and served either cold or hot as a table condiment in Cuban cooking.

Mustard Seed: the seeds of an Asian plant in the brassicus family. It is used in East Indian cooking and also as the base for prepared mustard.

Nutmeg: seeds of a southern Asian evergreen tree, native to the Spice Islands. The seed is grated and has a highly aromatic citrus and sweet flavor. It is used in desserts and potato dishes as well as a seasoning for vegetables.

Oregano: a member of the mint family, it means "joy of the mountain" in Greek. It is used extensively in Italian cooking and is similar in taste to marjoram, though not as sweet, and more powerful.

Paprika: dried and ground Spanish red peppers. It may be either hot or sweet and is used extensively in Hungarian and Spanish cuisine.

Parsley: one of the most widely used herbs in the world. It has a slightly peppery flavor and is cultivated on every continent except Antarctica. Used to season Spanish, Greek, Italian, and American dishes. It is used extensively for garnish. The two most common varieties are curly leaf, used mostly for garnish, and flat leaf or Italian Parsley as it is known in the US.

Peppercorns: seeds of the piper nigrum plant. Sold as white (mature, peeled), black (immature, unpeeled) or green (immature, unpeeled, and unaged). Very spicy hot when ground, it is extremely common and is used to season dishes of all types.

Pickling Spice: a blend of dried herbs and spices, usually whole, that is used to pickle a variety of vegetables and also to prepare corned beef. Mixtures vary but common ingredients are coriander, bay leaf, allspice, and mustard seed.

Rosemary: a member of the mint family, it is very durable and has a pronounced piney flavor. Used in Greek and Italian cooking, especially for seasoning lamb.

Safflower: also called Mexican saffron. It is used mostly as a cheaper substitute for saffron, the world's most expensive spice. The oil from the seeds is the highest in unsaturated and also has a high smoke point, making it ideal for stir-frying.

Saffron: stigmas of the Chinese Crocus flower; it is the world's most expensive spice. It takes up to ten thousand flowers to produce one pound of saffron. Used in ancient times for medicinal purposes as well as cooking. It imparts a pronounced yellow-orange color to foods like bouillabaisse and paella. Should be soaked in liquid before use.

Sage: a Mediterranean herb with a musty and somewhat bitter flavor. It is used in savory sauces, butters, and most frequently in America as an ingredient in roast turkey stuffing.

Sambal Ulek: also called sambal oelek. The most basic of a series of spices used as multi-purpose condiments in Malaysian and Indonesian cooking. Usually a combination of chilies, brown sugar, and salt. Other sambals are more complex. Sometimes combined with coconut milk for sauces or served as a table condiment for curries and rice.

Savory: there are two varieties—summer and winter. A member of the mint family, it has a flavor that is similar to mint and thyme. Used in pates, soups, and sauces.

Shallot: a member of the alium family. It has a milder flavor than garlic but heartier than onion. It is used extensively in French cooking for sauces, and vegetable, meat, and fish dishes.

Sorrel: a member of the buckwheat family, it is used to flavor omelets, cream soups, and vegetable dishes. It is very high in oxalic acid, which accounts for its bitter flavor.

Star Anise: a member of the magnolia family, it is not related to anise although it is similar in flavor. It comes from a small Asian evergreen tree and is one of the components of Chinese five spice.

Szechwan Peppercorn: a spicy berry of the Chinese prickly ash tree. It has an aromatic citrus flavor that is used to spice many dishes from the province it is named after.

Tarragon: a key ingredient in Béarnaise Sauce. It has a slight licorice flavor and is used extensively in French cooking to season sauces, seafood, and vegetables.

Thyme: a member of the mint family, it has a pungent, somewhat lemony flavor and is used in Italian and Greek cooking to season sauces, vegetables, and meat. It is one of the ingredients in bouquet garni.

Turmeric: the ground-dried root of the plant of the same name, related to ginger. Its bright yellow color is used to both season and color Indian dishes. It is what gives prepared mustard its characteristic yellow color.

Vanilla: the flowery pods of a type of tropical orchid. It is one of the most widely used spices in baking and dessert cooking. Native to Madagascar, Mexico, and Tahiti, the "beans" can be quite expensive. Most frequently, alcoholic extracts are used in home baking.

Za'atar: in its pure form it is a native Middle Eastern herb with a flavor similar to marjoram, oregano, and thyme. It means "thyme" in Arabic and is sometimes called Syrian marjoram. Za'atar (also spelled zahtar) is also a blend of herbs, usually toasted sesame seeds, sumac, thyme, and marjoram, used to infuse olive oil for drizzling over bread.

APPENDIX TWO

Abbreviations Used in this Book

Unit	Abbreviation
Teaspoon	t.
Tablespoon	T.
Cup	c.
Pint	pt.
Quart	qt.
Gallon	gal.
Ounce	oz.
Pound	lb.
Gram	g.
Kilogram	k.

APPENDIX THREE

Conversions of Weights and Measures

VOLUMETRIC CONVERSIONS

Teaspoons	Tablespoons	Fluid Ounces	Cups	Quarts
3	1	½	—	—
6	2	1	⅛	—
12	4	2	¼	—
24	8	4	½	—
—	12	6	¾	—
—	16	8	1	¼
—	—	16	2	½
—	—	32	4	1

WEIGHT CONVERSIONS

Grams	Ounces	Pounds
28	1	0.06
57	2	0.13
114	4	0.25
227	8	0.50
454	16	1.00
1000 (1 Kg.)	35	2.2

References

1. *All About Sweet Corn*; Cuisine at Home; Issue no. 34, pp.18; Aug. 2002.
2. Herbst, Sharon Tyler; *Food Lover's Companion*; *Barron's*; Hauppage, NY; 2001.
3. Herrmann Loomis, Susan; *The Great American Seafood Cookbook*; Workman Publishing; N.Y.C., NY; 1988.
4. White, Jasper; *Lobster at Home*; Scribner; N.Y.C., NY; 1998.
5. Edwards, J. P.; *Simply "Mah-velous" Cooking—The Science and Art of Cooking Without Recipes*; Food & Fun; Chef Zetti's Gourmet Foods; Houston, TX; 1994
6. Harvey Lang, Jennifer; *LaRousse Gastronomique*; Crown Publishers; N.Y.C., NY; 1988.
7. Wickizer, V. D. and Bennett, M. K.; *The Rice Economy of Monsoon Asia*; Stanford University Press; Palo Alto, CA.; 1941.
8. Dowell, Phillip and Bailey, Adrian; *Cook's Ingredients*; Bantam Books; New York, Toronto, London; 1980.
9. foodtelevision network.com
10. http://lamar.colostate.edu/~samcox/Tomato.html
11. *ServSafe Essential*; National Restaurant Association Educational Foundation; 2002.
12 *Hazard Analysis Report*; NJ State Department of Health, Consumer Health Services; Trenton, NJ, 08625

13. *Hazard Analysis Critical Control Point*; Bergen County Department of Health Services; Oradell, NJ
14. www.thedailygreen.com
15. Vegetarian/vegan food pyramid developed by the Department of Nutrition, Arizona State University, Art by Nick Rickert.
16. www.eatright.org
17. www.vegsoc.org
18. American Dietetic Association, *Becoming Vegetarian*, Chicago, Illinois, 2007
19. Walters, Terry; *Clean Food—A Seasonal Guide to Eating Close to the Source*; Sterling Publishing; NY, NY; 2007.
20. www.epicurious.com
21. Wikipedia.com
22. Ryan, Tim, C.M.C. et al; *The Professional Chef*; 7th Edition; John Wiley and Sons; N.Y.C., NY; 2002
23. Barr, Tracy; *Cast Iron Cooking For Dummies*; Wiley Publishing; Hoboken, NJ; 2004.
24. Ryan, Tim, C.M.C. *et al*; *The Professional Chef*; 7th Edition; John Wiley and Sons; N.Y.C., NY; 2002
25 Child, Julia; *The Way to Cook*; Alfred A. Knopf; N.Y.C., NY; 1989
26. Food Network.com
27. www.epicurious.com
28. Television Food Network; 2003.
29. Westmoreland, Susan, ed.; *Good Housekeeping Great American Classics Cookbook*; Hearst Books; NY, NY; 2004
30. Batali, Mario; *Molto Italiano*; Harper Collins; NY, NY; 2005
31. Hess, Reinhardt; Schinharl, Cornelia and Salzer, Sabine; *The New Regional Italian Cookbook*; Barrons; Hauppauge, NY; 2006.
32. Prudhomme, Paul; *Chef Paul Prudhomme's Louisiana Kitchen*; William and Morrow Company, Inc; New York, NY; 1984.
33. Career.kent.edu/home/res/images/Dining.gifcareer.kent.edu/home/res/images/Dining.gif
34. www.emilypost.com/gfx/formal_place_setting.gifwww.emilypost.com/gfx/formal_place_setting.gif
35. *Salad Dressings Revived*; Cuisine at Home; Issue No. 34; Aug. 2002; p. 23.
36. Willaimson, Sarah; *Kids Cook*; Williamson Publishing; Charlotte, Vermont; 1992.

Index

Acknowledgements

I wish to acknowledge the following people for their contributions in the making of this book. First, to my wonderfully talented photographer and friend Ted Axelrod, whose photos have brought my food to life. To my lifelong buddy and talented artist Phil Felix, whose freehand illustrations belong in a museum. To my siblings and biggest fans—my brother Joe, and sisters Maria, Luci, and Patty. They have put up with so much from me throughout the years and somehow they've managed to stick by me. To my amazing family of friends in Texas—Susan, Susan, Sean, RD, Debbie, Lloyd, Diane, Anita, Kasi, Stacy, Jenny, Jeff, Marie, Tom, Julie, Bob, Dan, Mona, Peaches, Michael, and all those who have opened their homes and hearts to me whenever I show up. To my equally amazing family of friends in Florida—Larry, Judi, Eric, Gary, J. Lew, Izzy, Robert, Eddie, Patty, and all those who have allowed me to trash their kitchens for the past twenty years under the guise of a Super Bowl Party. To my friends and fans Eric, Arwen, Mike, Mike, Leo, Danny, and the entire Kiku gang for their support and encouragement. A special thanks to Greg Jeu, who gave me my start as a professional writer in 1985. A very special thanks to my family of friends at Chef Central. You are too numerous to list by name and I know if I tried to do so, I would probably leave someone out. It was an incredible eighteen-year journey, during which time we created something special that will never be repeated in quite the same way. Along with our collaborators from outside the company, we created a litany of events that will stand the test of time with respect to relevance. It was my privilege to be a part of the adventure for the past fifteen years.

Finally and most importantly, I wish to thank my mother, Anna, a vested member of the Greatest Generation of Americans. She grew up during the Great Depression, when she learned about sacrifice and survival. She answered the call of her country by enlisting in the Army during World War II. She served honorably, reaching the rank of First Lieutenant. She raised a family of five children, largely as a single mother. She sacrificed everything for her children—they just don't make them like her anymore. I love you, Mom.